i

Contents

Figures

> *With mission assurance utmost in mind, this handbook is intended to provide an installation commander & staff with a generalized approach to eliminate, minimize, or otherwise mitigate risks to the mission as posed by Industrial Control System (ICS) vulnerabilities.*

> "The most common cause of task degradation or mission failure is human error, specifically the inability to consistently manage risk."
>
> *OPNAVINST 3500.39C (2010), para. 4*

iv

Industrial Control Systems
Vulnerability & Risk Self-Assessment Aid

EXECUTIVE SUMMARY

Key Points
- The primary goal is mission assurance.
- The primary focus is on risk management.
- The primary audience is the installation commander, with his or her staff as close secondary.
- The primary intent is to facilitate self-assessment of Industrial Control Systems (ICS) security posture vis-à-vis missions' priorities.
- The primary approach is generic, enabling broad (Joint/all Services) utility.

One of the essential responsibilities of the installation commander and supporting staff is to manage risks to establish optimal conditions for assuring successful accomplishment of assigned missions every day. Although not always obvious, many missions depend on the unfailing functioning of ICS and therefore on the security of those systems.

A mission assured today is never taken for granted as assured tomorrow. Mission assurance demands constant vigilance along with proactive risk management. Risks come in myriad shapes and sizes—some enduring, some sporadic and situational, others appearing without warning. ICS represent only one set among a vast array of mission vulnerabilities and risks, an array that often competes for resources and, therefore, requires prioritization of management actions.

This handbook is intended for use primarily by Department of Defense (DOD) installation commanders, supported by staff members, as a **management tool** to <u>self-assess,</u>[1] prioritize, and manage mission-related vulnerabilities and risks that may be exposed or created by connectivity to ICS. ICS include a variety of systems or mechanisms used to monitor and/or operate critical infrastructure elements, such as electricity, water, natural gas, fuels, entry and access (doors, buildings, gates), heating & air-conditioning, runway lighting, etc. Other terms

---

[1] Other entities and programs are available to conduct formal and very thorough technical assessments, but those must be coordinated, scheduled, and resourced (i.e., funded). This aid provides an ability to conduct self-assessments when/as necessary or desired, and thereby, also the ability to prioritize and manage the resources required to address identified vulnerabilities and risks.

often heard include SCADA, DCS, or EMCS.[2] Throughout this book the term "ICS" is used as encompassing such variations.

This book is intentionally <u>generic</u>. Whatever the category of ICS, the *approach* to vulnerability assessment and risk management is similar. The applicability of actions recommended here may be extended to any DOD military installation regardless of the specific categories of ICS encountered. In keeping with the generic approach and due primarily to the unique nature of each installation's infrastructure, beyond a couple of exceptions there are no checklists, standard operating procedures (SOP), or similar sets of lock-step actions provided here. However, a risk management team using the handbook likely will want to develop checklists tailored to their specific circumstances.

Among other purposes, this handbook is intended to increase awareness of how a threat related to the ICS itself translates into a threat to the mission, either directly through the ICS or circuitously via network connections. Every military installation has numerous mission-support processes and systems controlled by, or that otherwise depend on, ICS. Every connection or access point represents potential vulnerabilities and, therefore, risks to the system under control (i.e., electrical, water, emergency services, etc.), which can escalate quickly to adverse impact on mission essential functions (MEF) and mission accomplishment.

Fundamentally then, this handbook is provided to help the installation leadership conduct a risk self-assessment focused on ICS and supported missions and then implement plans to manage that risk. Most of the information contained herein is not unique to this publication. <u>Two unique aspects</u> are: (1) the aggregation of disparate information into one place, distilling essentials, and tailoring to DOD installation leadership; and (2) bringing cyber/information technology (IT), civil engineers, public works, and mission operators together with a singular focus on ICS security in support of missions. This handbook (via Appendices) also points to additional resources.

The <u>key set of activities</u>—one exception to the "no checklists" approach—is found under the heading "<u>ICS Security Assessment Process</u>." Succinctly the process consists of eight steps, which if implemented with deliberation and in a team environment, will set the success conditions for all other actions recommended or suggested within this handbook (see <u>Figure 1</u>). This set of eight steps represents the core of the handbook. **All other information herein is intended to support implementation of those eight steps.**

---

[2] SCADA= Supervisory Control and Data Acquisition; DCS = Distributed Control System; EMCS = Energy Management Control System. Other variations exist; for example, building control systems.

Before explaining the eight-step assessment process, the handbook provides introductory, informative and supporting information. Closely aligned with and serving as companion to the "Assessment Process" is a section titled "Framework for Successful ICS Defense." If the installation does not already have a single ICS manager and/or team, the "Framework" should be considered prior to engaging on the eight-step process.

- **Analyze Missions**
- Prioritize missions

Step 1

- **Identify Assets**
- Inventory; map; visually inspect

Step 2

- **Determine ICS Connectivity**
- All connection points, incl. potential

Step 3

- **Determine ICS Dependencies**
- Link missions, assets, infrastructure, ICS

Step 4

- **Assess Risk to Mission**
- Threats, vulnerabilities, consequences

Step 5

- **Prioritize Risk Mgmt Approaches**
- Based on mission prioritizes and resources

Step 6

- **Implement Actions**
- Commit resources; assign responsibilities

Step 7

- **Monitor & Reassess**
- Continuous process; not "one-and-done"

Step 8

Figure 1. ICS Security Assessment Eight-Step Process

INDUSTRIAL CONTROL SYSTEMS "101"

Key Point

- Understanding ICS is not difficult; the challenge is to understand the ICS relationship to missions.

Fundamentally Industrial Control Systems (ICS) are systems and mechanisms that control flow. ICS control flow of electricity, fluids, gases, air, traffic, and even people. They are the computer-controlled electro-mechanical systems that ensure installation infrastructure services are delivered when and where required to accomplish the mission. In the electric infrastructure, they control actions such as opening and closing switches; for water, they open and close valves; for buildings, they control access to various doors as well as operation of the heating, ventilation, and air conditioning (HVAC) system.

The term "Industrial Control System" is broad; specific instances of ICS may be called Supervisory Control and Data Acquisition (SCADA), Distributed Control System (DCS), Energy Management Control System (EMCS), Emergency Medical Service (EMS), or other terms but all perform the same fundamental function. Also, on DOD installations, ICS are associated primarily with infrastructure elements; therefore, though not technically accurate, they may be referred to as "Infrastructure" vice "Industrial" control systems. The hardware components that comprise an ICS usually are classed as operational technology (OT) versus information technology (IT), which refers to (among other things) the computer equipment that sits on nearly every desk. Another term used in this domain is Platform Information Technology (PIT),[3] (and PITI, with the 'I' referring to interconnect, or connected to the network) although ICS are only one sub-category of PIT, which also includes weapons systems, aircraft, vehicles, buildings, etc. Terminology is not that critical. What is important is to know that ICS are critical to the mission.

You frequently have used an ICS—though not by that term—in your home. It is called a "thermostat." The most simple of thermostats may not be so obvious as an ICS, but the more sophisticated can be programmed to automatically control the flow of air (heated, cooled, or just fan) by day, time, room, zone, etc. The most advanced allow the owner to monitor and operate the system over an Internet connection or Wi-Fi, using a Smartphone or tablet.

The "Smart Grid," once fully implemented, will allow your utility company to operate your thermostat remotely. The thermostat monitors temperatures (and some include humidity) and

---

[3] "PIT" is used more by the Air Force and to a lesser extent by the Navy. At the DoD level, PIT is addressed mostly under information assurance (IA) guidance, such as DODI 8500.2. See the Glossary for a DOD definition of PIT.

then operates the electro-mechanical equipment (furnace, air conditioner, fan) to respond to the preset conditions you have selected. If the thermostat fails—even though the mechanicals are in perfect operating condition—the mission (cool, heat) fails. This same concept translates to the installation's missions: if the ICS fails the mission can fail, although the direct cause and effect may not always be so obvious.

ICS typically are not visible to the general population. The control devices themselves are behind panels, behind walls, inside cabinets, under floors, under roads; the master control computers more often reside in a room in a civil engineer (CE) or public works (PW) facility. Because they are essentially invisible to all but CE and PW, and are considered as simply infrastructure elements, ICS often are overlooked when assessing mission dependencies. Regardless of where they physically reside or who directly operates the ICS, every person and every mission on the installation is a stakeholder in their properly functioning.

While the ICS field (vs. control room) elements consist of mostly electro-mechanical devices, some are actually computers that control other field devices and communicate with other computers in the system with minimal human interaction. The most common example of this type is the Programmable Logic Controller (PLC).[4] PLCs (and their cousins, Remote Terminal Units or RTU) are very important because they are <u>computers</u>, typically not under direct human supervision, and offer multiple pathways (e.g., wireless, modem, Ethernet, Universal Serial Bus [USB]) for connecting to <u>both</u> the controlled infrastructure and the network. This combination of characteristics makes the PLC an especially vulnerable node in the ICS.

At the front end—the control center—is where most of the computers (servers, system interfaces, etc.) and, more critically, **connection** to other networks reside. While PLCs/RTUs may become connected (autonomously or by human intervention) for intermittent periods, control center computers may be <u>continuously connected</u>[5] to the Non-secure Internet Protocol Router Network (NIPRNet), other elements of the Global Information Grid (GIG), and/or an Internet Service Provider (ISP). It is especially at this node that ICS should be treated with the same security considerations as with IT.

Whether an ICS element is continuously or only intermittently connected presents the same fundamental security issue. Anytime an element is connected to a network, even if for only

---

[4] Many will recall that a Siemens PLC was the primary target for the Stuxnet code that impacted the centrifuges in the Iranian nuclear processing facility at Natanz in 2010. This same PLC (or variants) can be found in the critical infrastructures on numerous DOD installations. See an informative Wikipedia article on Stuxnet here: http://en.wikipedia.org/wiki/Stuxnet

[5] Another term used here is PIT-I, or PIT-Interconnect—that juncture where the ICS (or OT) connects with the IT network. For detail on PIT and PIT-I, in addition to DODI 8500.2, see: DODD 8500.01E; AFI 33-210 with AFGM2.2; AFCESA ETL 11-1; DON CIO Memo 02-10 and Enclosures.

brief instances, it is vulnerable to destructive attack, compromise, or manipulation. Therefore, when assessing risk the **key question** is not "Is it connected?" but "Is it connect-<u>able</u>?" Network mapping (via software) will <u>not</u> reveal such potential connectivity; only a physical, visual inspection of an element by a knowledgeable expert (more likely an IT than a CE or PW person) will yield specific information on what type of connection ports exist on what elements. Where the location of an element makes visual inspection impractical or impossible, use the manufacturer's or vendor's published manuals for that specific piece of equipment.

Understanding the fundamentals of ICS is not difficult. The challenge is in understanding the dependencies of mission on ICS and therefore, appropriately managing the risks to the ICS and to the missions they support. This handbook is intended to assist the commander and staff in gaining that understanding.

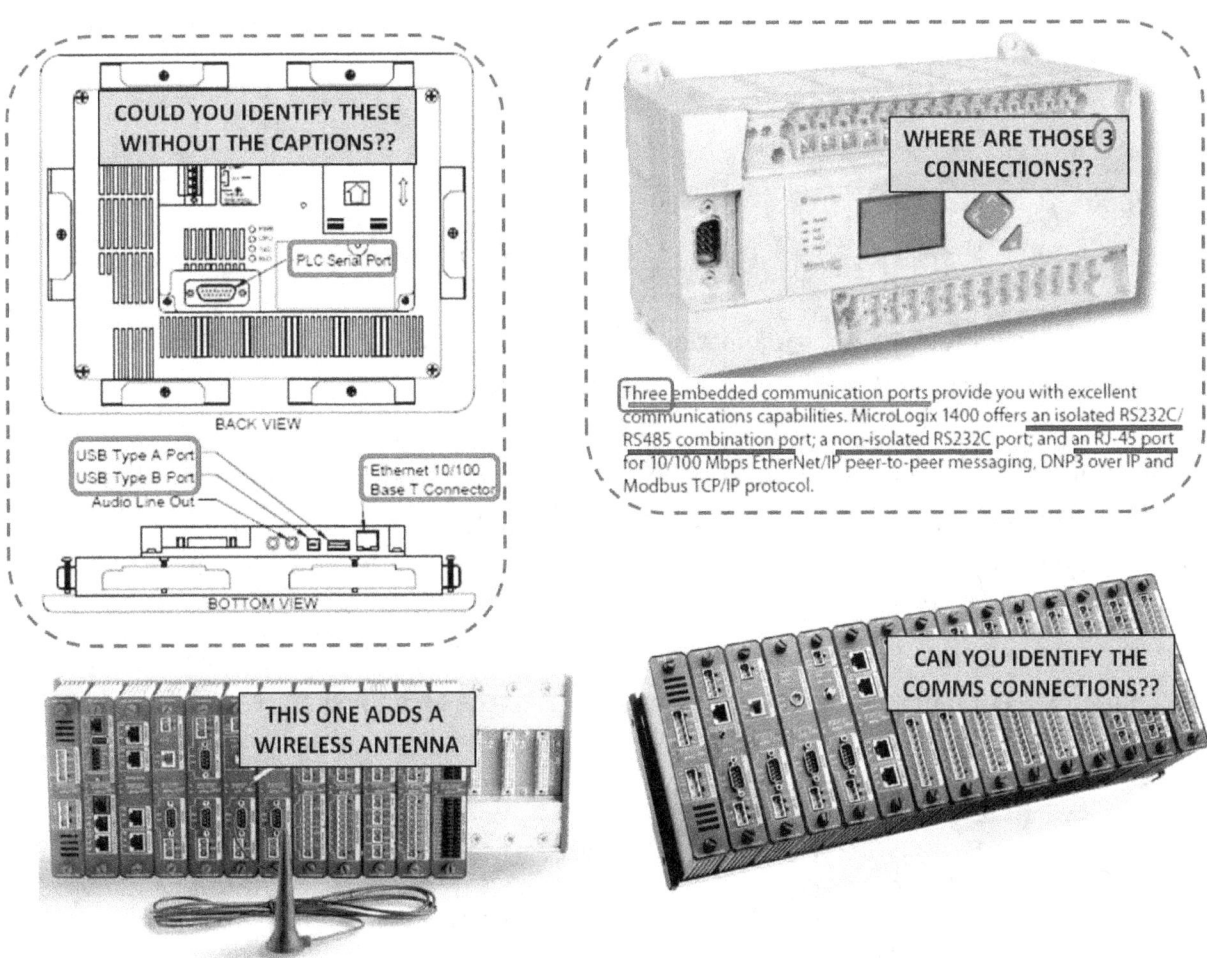

Figure 2. PLCs & RTUs: The Challenge of Finding the Connectivity

HANDBOOK AUTHORITIES

Key Point:
- The handbook reflects breadth and depth of ICS community expertise.

This handbook was developed based on a broad collection of authoritative sources;[6] underwent field testing to validate the framework and applicability at the installation command level; was reviewed by a Joint Warfighter Advisory Group (JWAG[7]) to verify broad (i.e., Joint) applicability; and received direct input by a broad-based selection of ICS and risk management subject matter experts (SME). Users of this handbook will gain even greater value by referencing current publications of primary sources. Some of the major publications are listed in Appendix A, <u>References</u>. Note that while this handbook is advisory, many of the sources are authoritative and/or directive.

DISTINCTIONS BETWEEN ICS AND IT

Key Point:
- ICS and IT share similarities, but also have unique characteristics.

Fundamentally ICS security is a combination of IA, cyber security, physical security, and operations security (OPSEC). This same combination is applicable to IT, so is there any difference between ICS and IT? Yes. One key distinction between ICS and other IT architectures is that the physical world can be impacted disastrously by malicious (or only accidental) manipulation of the ICS. For example, with IT there typically is linkage with only other IT components; with ICS the linkage can be to the electric grid, powering other critical assets, as well as to other infrastructure elements. This gives rise to another primary distinction, namely that ICS must always be available while "pure" IT can survive downtimes. Another important difference is in the "refresh" rates of the technologies: IT tends to turn over in three years or less while OT (ICS) can be on a 20-year cycle. Why is this important to know?

---

[6] Among sources: Idaho National Laboratory (INL); AF Civil Engineer Support Agency (AFCESA); Department of Homeland Security DHS ICS-Computer Emergency Response Team (CERT); the National SCADA Test Bed (NSTB); DHS Center for the Protection of National Infrastructure (CPNI); National Institute of Standards and Technology (NIST); National Security Agency's (NSA) Committee on National Security Systems (CNSS); Federal Information Processing Standards (FIPS); and numerous SMEs who are members of or closely associated with the DoD.

[7] JWAG participants may differ from meeting-to-meeting, but broadly represent stakeholders in the outcome or product of a specified Joint activity or project. For this handbook the initial JWAG included representatives from United States Cyber Command (USCYBERCOM), Northern Command (NORTHCOM), AFCESA, INL, Sandia National Laboratory (SNL), and various CE and communications experts from both Army and Air Force elements of Joint Base San Antonio.

The long refresh cycle of ICS results in hardware, software, and operating systems no longer supported by vendors. The impacts of lack of support include: woefully stale malware detection programs, operating systems that cannot handle newer (and more efficient/effective) software programs, and hardware that may be on the verge of catastrophic failure with no backup or failover equipment available.

The following extract from NIST Special Publication 800-82[8] provides an excellent review of not only the distinctions but also the similarities and how OT (such as ICS) and IT are converging.

> "Initially, ICS had little resemblance to traditional information technology (IT) systems in that ICS were isolated systems running proprietary control protocols using specialized hardware and software. Widely available, low-cost Internet Protocol (IP) devices are now replacing proprietary solutions, which increases the possibility of cyber security vulnerabilities and incidents. As ICS are adopting IT solutions to promote corporate business systems connectivity and remote access capabilities, and are being designed and implemented using industry standard computers, operating systems (OS) and network protocols, they are starting to resemble IT systems. This integration supports new IT capabilities, but it provides significantly less isolation for ICS from the outside world than predecessor systems, creating a greater need to secure these systems. While security solutions have been designed to deal with these security issues in typical IT systems, special precautions must be taken when introducing these same solutions to ICS environments. In some cases, new security solutions are needed that are tailored to the ICS environment.

> "Although some characteristics are similar, ICS also have characteristics that differ from traditional information processing systems. Many of these differences stem from the fact that logic executing in ICS has a direct affect on the physical world. Some of these characteristics include significant risk to the health and safety of human lives and serious damage to the environment, as well as serious financial issues such as production losses, negative impact to a nation's economy, and compromise of proprietary information. ICS have unique performance and reliability requirements and often use operating systems and applications that may be considered unconventional to typical IT personnel. Furthermore, the goals of safety and efficiency sometimes conflict with security in the design and operation of control systems.

---

[8] NIST SP 800-82, 2011 version, Executive Summary, p.1.

Originally, ICS implementations were susceptible primarily to local threats because many of their components were in physically secured areas and the components were not connected to IT networks or systems. However, the trend toward integrating ICS systems with IT networks provides significantly less isolation for ICS from the outside world than predecessor systems, creating a greater need to secure these systems from remote, external threats. Also, the increasing use of wireless networking places ICS implementations at greater risk from adversaries who are in relatively close physical proximity but do not have direct physical access to the equipment. Threats to control systems can come from numerous sources, including hostile governments, terrorist groups, disgruntled employees, malicious intruders, complexities, accidents, natural disasters as well as malicious or accidental actions by insiders. ICS security objectives typically follow the priority of availability, integrity and confidentiality, in that order."

Distinctions between ICS and IT aside, from a purely technical security standpoint, ICS may be considered on par with IT or IA vis-à-vis security challenges, albeit with warnings about use of certain software tools on the networks.[9]

THREATS

Key Point:
- Threats are global but assessments must be local.

What threats could be posed to an installation's mission by or through the ICS? This is an essential question, but one that cannot be answered specifically in an unclassified venue or simplistically in any venue. Generically, threats fall into categories similar to IT and/or cyber: terrorist, criminal, insider, environmental, etc. Use of this self-assessment handbook can lead to a deeper understanding of the infrastructure and establish mitigation conditions whereby specific threats may be identified. But even without specific threats known many risks can be

---

[9] Caveat emptor with respect to software tools. Software applications that test, penetrate, scan, characterize, and/or defend networks should be considered equivalent to "loaded weapons" with respect to control systems. Some tools that are entirely "safe" when used on IT networks have been demonstrated both in the field and under controlled conditions to have negative, even catastrophic effects on ICS networks. If such tools are considered for use on ICS, the decision must be an informed one and the tool operator must be a SME who understands potential effects of that tool on an ICS. Furthermore, any such use must be coordinated with the relevant IT agency (e.g., Service CERT) because tool use on the connected ICS could trip various IT network defense mechanisms (firewalls, intrusion detection system (IDS), intrusion prevention system (IPS), etc).

identified and managed. In other words, this handbook can help to establish a more effective and efficient security posture to conduct formal threat assessments.

The Security Incidents Organization in a 2009 survey (not specific to DOD) assessed that roughly 75% of ICS incidents were unintentional. Of the 25% that were intentional, over half were by insiders. In other words, external threat actors were responsible for events only about 10% of the time. <u>Based on percentages alone</u>, the hostile threat actor would *appear* to be of far less concern than a mistake committed by a legitimate operator. However, the external threat actor represents a potentially far more malicious and far-reaching impact on mission than either the intentional insider or unintentional event. Among external threats, perhaps the most insidious is the so-called Advanced Persistent Threat, or APT. The National Institute of Standards and Technology (NIST) (*et al*) assesses that the external threat actor found ways not only to get "inside" but also to stay there as long as he wants or needs. The APT,[10] especially nation-state sponsored, is perhaps the most ominous threat to DOD networks. Open source information on threats is plentiful and readily available, but ICS security teams will need access to classified intelligence resources to obtain more "actionable" information.

> "The increasing interconnectivity and interdependence among commercial and defense infrastructures demand that DOD take steps to understand and remedy or mitigate the vulnerabilities of, and threats to, the critical infrastructures on which it depends for mission accomplishment."
>
> *Joint Pub 3-27 (p. VII-8)*

MISSION PRIORITIES

Key Points:
- Missions are interconnected and mutually dependent in complex ways.
- Priorities tend to be situational and event-driven.

The US Navy, articulating what is essentially true for all the Services and including ICS as part of their cyber infrastructure, has stated:[11]

> "The Department of the Navy (DON) relies on a network of physical and cyber infrastructure so critical that its degradation, exploitation, or destruction could have a debilitating effect on the DON's ability to project, support, and sustain its forces and operations worldwide. This critical infrastructure includes DON and non-DON domestic and foreign

---

[10] NIST addressed the APT in Revision 4 to SP 800-53.
[11] *Critical Infrastructure Protection Program, Strategy for 2009 and Beyond*, 2009

infrastructures essential to planning, mobilizing, deploying, executing, and sustaining U.S. military operations on a global basis. Mission Assurance is a process to ensure that assigned tasks or duties can be performed in accordance with the intended purpose or plan. It is made more difficult due to increased interconnectivity and interdependency of systems and networks. DON critical infrastructures, both physical and cyber, even if degraded, must be available to meet the requirements of multiple, dynamic, and divergent missions."

> "Major ship systems may be impacted by SCADA network attacks ashore and afloat. This may impact a ship's ability to start or stop engines remotely disabling portions of the propulsion system and other engineering systems."
>
> *Navy TACMEMO NWDC 3-56.1-12*

Which ICS receive greater focus for security efforts will depend in most cases on what missions they support. The 262d Network Warfare Squadron (262 NWS) defines this as the "criticality" of the system component whereby lesser systems may receive little to no focus while very critical and centralized systems are recommended to be hardened and protected significantly. An example might be where it is impossible to protect every component on a network; focus would be on critical servers, in essence accepting the risk of an individual personal computer compromise so long as it can be isolated and secure operation of the critical server maintained.

But even on a given installation mission priorities—and the importance of the supporting control systems—can change quickly and without advance notice. Consider the following hypothetical scenario highlighting such a rapid change.

Daedalus Air Force Base's primary mission is undergraduate pilot training. Flight operations are essential to this training. Flight operations depend on, among other things, a well-managed fuels system and properly functioning airfield lighting—both systems controlled by ICS. Therefore securing the lighting and fuels ICS networks will be a priority over, for example, automobile traffic control systems elsewhere on the installation. At 1430 on Thursday, a terrorist incident results in declaration of Force Protection Condition (FPCON) DELTA. At 1431 the primary mission of the installation dramatically shifts from UPT to defense (of people, infrastructure, and physical assets). ICS that are essential now include vehicular traffic control (not so critical under FPCON ALPHA) and emergency services (including camera systems, alarms, door controls, EMS and fire department dispatch, etc.). As a result of the incident, one of the ICS was damaged. The ICS maintainer is a commercial contractor whose facilities are not on the base. The contractor has backups of the ICS operating system, programs and data, but all are at the contractor facility off base. Because of the elevated FPCON, the contractor cannot enter the base. CE can provide some limited manual operation of the system, but is neither capable nor prepared to operate at even 50% efficiency and effectiveness.

Is the installation prepared for departures from the norm where ICS are part of the equation? Do the various existing installation plans (incident response, disaster recovery, installation emergency management, etc.) encompass ICS contingencies and emergencies? If so, have such contingencies been exercised (not simply "white-carded" during an exercise)? These are some of the considerations that will prove foundational to identifying ICS security priorities relative to missions and changing mission priorities.

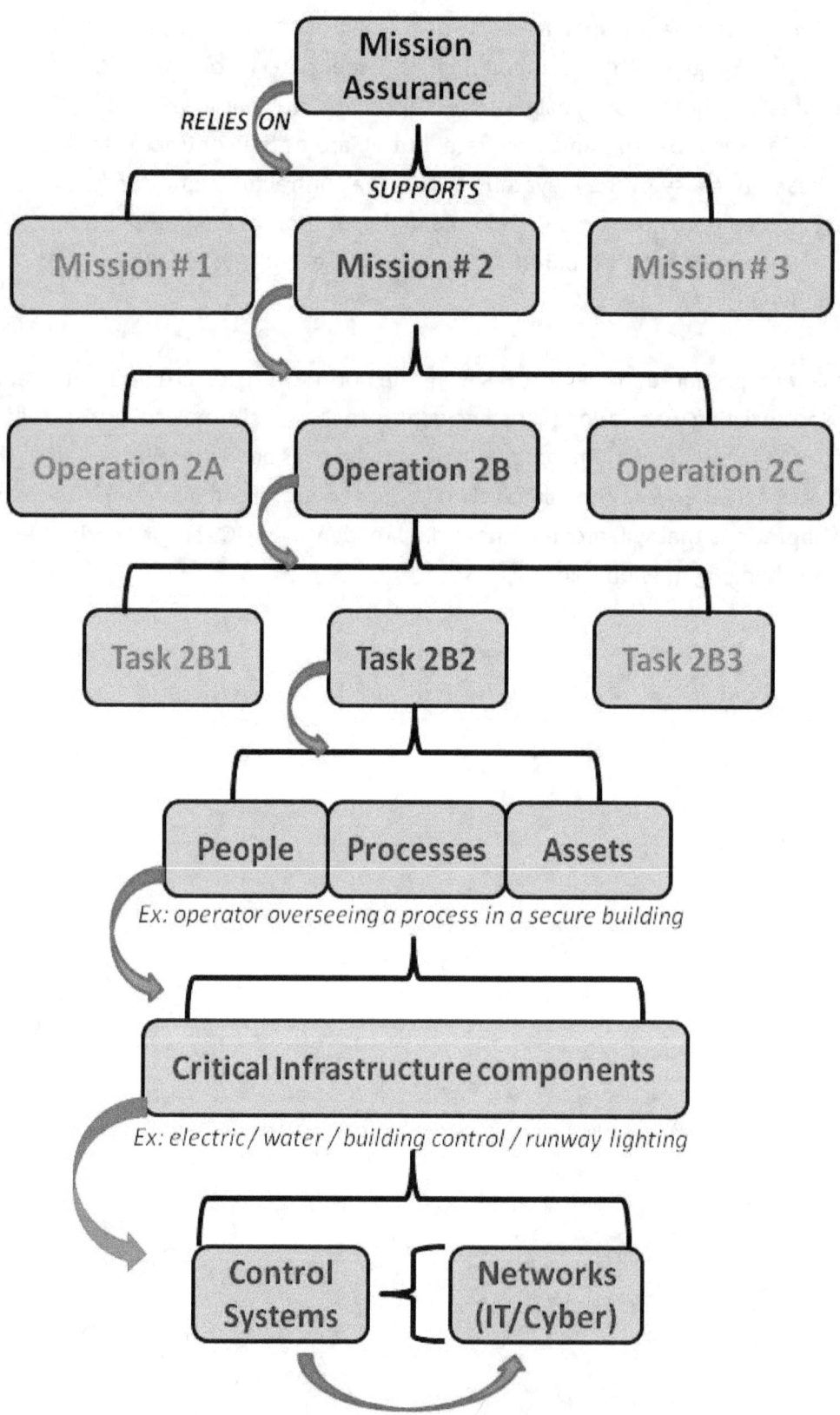

Figure 3. Mapping Mission Assurance to ICS

MISSION IMPACT

Key Point:
- If an element of the ICS and/or controlled infrastructure is compromised, critical mission functions may be degraded or even entirely failed.

For any installation commander, mission assurance is of utmost concern. Anything that may impact the mission rises to the top of the priority list. ICS and the controlled critical infrastructure are deemed to be mission enablers; damage to or compromise of ICS can degrade, compromise, or even deny the mission. With mission assurance foremost in mind, this handbook provides the installation commander with a generalized approach to eliminate, minimize, or otherwise mitigate risks to the mission as posed by ICS vulnerabilities.

It is important to note that this handbook does not attempt to achieve a level of specificity that addresses vulnerabilities of specific products from specific vendors in specific applications. Nor does it capture the range of threat actors who may be seeking to exploit those vulnerabilities. Such level of specificity must be addressed on a case-by-case basis under the collaborative efforts of the installation commander, CEs or PWs, communications element, and mission operations representatives, and, in some cases, external experts. Specifically for the threat piece of the equation, intelligence and/or law enforcement entities also must be consulted.

It is vitally important to understand that some mission-impacting vulnerabilities can be created at nodes where it may not be intuitively obvious. For example, consider a fuels control system directly supporting an operational mission. If this mission is assessed as high-priority, then the fuels control system (i.e., ICS) merits a commensurately high priority for defensive measures and may in fact be well defended. However there may be interconnections from non-mission-related systems linked back into those that are critical, opening paths of access to even defended nodes. For instance, there may be an unclassified IT network connection to the vehicle traffic control system, which in turn has a connection to the EMS management system, which in turn has a connection into the fuels management system. To discover which control systems may present vulnerabilities to the mission requires following the trail (virtually, logically, and physically) of <u>all</u> nodes and elements and their <u>potential</u> connections[12] as well as actual ones.

The probability of a threat actor finding and traversing all such interconnections to create negative effects on the mission may not be high at a given moment, but threat actors

---

[12] "Connection" includes wired network, wireless, radio, modem, USB port, Ethernet port....<u>anything</u> that enables one element to connect to another.

continuously develop more advanced skills.[13] Though current probability of a successful attack may not be high, the advanced skill sets available to malicious actors combined with more freely available advanced exploitation tools, many of which are created with ICS attack components or even specifically for ICS, make this a serious threat. No system or sub-system can be overlooked or assumed secure simply because it <u>appears</u> isolated. It is important to also note that a vulnerability and risk assessment should consider not just primary effects on a system, but potential second—and even third—order effects. Succinctly stated, an ICS vulnerability and risk assessment should be supported by a thorough <u>mission effects assessment</u>.

Prioritization of defense measures and resource allocation requires more than a one-to-one matching with missions, but rather needs to be approached comprehensively. There is added

> "The purpose of the Air Force's Critical Infrastructure Program (CIP) is to ensure Air Force's ability to execute missions and capabilities that are essential to planning, mobilizing, deploying, executing, and sustaining military operations on a global basis."
>
> *Air Force Energy Plan 2010 (p. 19)*

complexity created by Joint Base administration where one Service's primary mission likely is not the same as that of the other Services. Take for example a fuel delivery control system on a Joint Base hosting both Air Force and Army missions. For efficiency and cost savings, the fuels delivery systems and automated control may be consolidated. Hypothetically, for this installation the Air Force's primary mission may be to launch sorties providing defense of the North American airspace while the Army's may be to train vehicle maintenance and repair. If the Army is lead agent for the Joint Base, do they consider the fuels system as the top priority ICS to protect? How will this be decided where three or <u>all</u> Services are included in a Joint Base structure? Such questions underscore the imperative for a comprehensive approach.

THE MOST SECURE ICS

Key Points:
- No ICS is 100% secure 100% of the time.
- Misconceptions → undetected or neglected vulnerabilities → unmanaged risk.

---

[13] For example, the ICS-CERT in Alert 12-046-01, February 2012, stated: "ICS-CERT is monitoring and responding to an increase in a combination of threat elements that increase the risk of control system attacks. These elements include Internet accessible configurations, vulnerability and exploit tool releases for ICS devices, and increased interest and activity by hacktivist groups and others."

An absolutely 100% vulnerability-free, risk-free ICS does not exist and likely will not. To be *nearly* invulnerable,[14] an ICS must not be connected to anything other than its own infrastructure elements. There also must be no potential method for external connections: USB ports, Ethernet ports, wireless access points, satellite radio, modems, etc. Additionally, there would have to be unassailable physical controls. However, vendors often need real-time access to the infrastructure, and operators cannot be in all places all the time, which typically is mitigated by remote access capability. Also, the ICS manufacturing industry favors connectivity especially for vendor maintenance. Further complicating the security task is DOD's "green" mandate to convert the electric infrastructure to the "Smart Grid," which depends on wireless connectivity.[15]

The following "Top ICS Security Misconceptions" were presented in "318 OSS/IN SCADA Threat Assessment Report".[16] Note that this list reflects ideas at a point in time and then only the top five are presented; there are other relevant misconceptions, and all will most certainly change over time. The point is simply that there is widespread misunderstanding about ICS security and that such misunderstanding can result in a less-than-secure system. For brevity, the "misconceptions" have been edited but retain the essential message of each as presented in the original report:

- Misconception 1: **ICS & SCADA Systems Have a Secure Software Profile**.

Discussion: Systems that manage the delivery of critical resources should be viewed as one of the nation's top security priorities. ICS has not yet achieved the same level of security concern as other cyber or IT resources. ICS typically are installed with *availability* as the primary driver and then operating efficiency and cost-effectiveness as secondary imperatives; robust security typically is an after-thought and sometimes not considered at all.

- Misconception 2: **ICS & SCADA Systems are Monitored by IT Professionals**.

Discussion: To those not directly involved it may seem that ICS falls under purview of the IT experts, but that typically is not the case. Most often CEs or PWs are responsible for not only the hardware elements of the infrastructure, but also the software and communications

---

[14] Complete invulnerability is unachievable especially where the human element is necessary—thus the insider threat is always a potential.

[15] For example, "demand-response" management by the EMCS connecting to any load (fuels, lighting, HVAC, whatever, wherever, whenever) depends on dedicated Internet connectivity. Military installations are implementing smart grid technology as microgrids. On the other hand and more optimistically there are a number of initiatives to enhance security for new (not legacy, though) systems such as the Advanced Metering Infrastructure (AMI).

[16] Classified report published June 2012. Portions reproduced here are marked unclassified in the source report.

(network) components. While many engineers receive IT training it is often not as extensive as for an IT professional, and typically centers on operational rather than security aspects.

- Misconception 3: **All ICS Systems are Air-Gapped and Therefore Secure.**

Discussion: Not only is this not true (and actually never was even when most systems were isolated), but more and more systems that *were* air-gapped are being connected. Even air-gapped[17] systems are vulnerable, as demonstrated acutely by Stuxnet. Typically air-gapped systems still have <u>connectable</u> access points, such as the USB drive in the Stuxnet case. Additionally, when upgrades are made they may be by a CD that has not been properly scanned for viruses or by a vendor plugging an unscanned laptop into an Ethernet port. Not only is "air gapped" not necessarily secure, but dangerously can create a false sense of security (lends to the "security by obscurity" fallacy). Yet another facet of this is that the "isolated" system often is overlooked or even intentionally ignored during security audits that focus on the IT or network elements.

- Misconception 4: **ICS & SCADA Systems are Physically Secure.**

Discussion: Perhaps most of those directly under control of DOD are physically secure (though that has been shown to be false numerous times), but those not under DOD control are less likely to be secure, at least to DOD standards. The Government Accountability Office (GAO) estimates that 85% of energy infrastructure is "outside the fence" and that 99% of DOD's energy needs are met by commercial providers. Physical security (or lack thereof) does not end at the fence. In other words, no matter how physically secure the installation may be there are still external risks to be addressed. DOD dependence on commercial owners and providers demands a teaming approach to physical security.

- Misconception 5: **Proprietary Protocols Offer Security Through Obscurity.**

Discussion: "Proprietary" serves as an impediment only to those operating legally and ethically, and to a certain extent unsophisticated bad actors (only because they had not yet acquired the skills). To the experienced hacker and state-sponsored actor, protocols are discoverable and exploitable. There even have been web-published revelations of proprietary protocols by so-called independent researchers.

Misconceptions abound; therefore security may never be assumed or taken for granted. Any given installation's "most secure" ICS is fundamentally a function of continuous risk assessment and management relative to given missions and situationally-dependent mission priorities.

---

[17] "Air Gap" refers to having no electronic connection, requiring data to be moved "by hand" from one system to another via media such as USB drives, CDs, etc.

Continuous awareness is key to recognizing vulnerabilities early and committing necessary resources to manage potential risks. Proactivity is fundamental.

RISK ASSESSMENT & MANAGEMENT

Key Point:

- Risk management is a continuous process.

Risk is a function of the interaction among threat,[18] vulnerability, and consequence (or mission impact). Risk management involves a process of understanding each element of the equation, how those elements interact, and how to respond to the assessed risk. Every installation will face an ever-changing threat-vulnerability-consequence equation. SMEs within DOD, Department of Energy (DOE), and industry agree that even the most secure network has, or will have, inherent vulnerabilities. Therefore risk management is essential and must be a continuous process rather than an *event* that takes place annually, quarterly, or even monthly. Risk management is not only continuous but is situational based on the relative uniqueness of each ICS infrastructure. Appendix F *provides examples of risk assessment models.*

FRAMEWORK FOR SUCCESSFUL ICS DEFENSE

Key Point:

- ICS defense is a team effort.

While there is no DOD, Joint, or Service policy or directive specific to creating a security program for installation ICS, numerous publications do provide some guidance and address elements of ICS security. The following "best practice" framework is derived from such guidance.

1. Appoint a full-time ICS Information Assurance Manager (IAM) specifically for installation control systems (i.e., distinct from an IT IAM).[19] As an on-going coordinator of a team formed in the next step, the ICS IAM[20] will be responsible specifically for ICS and should function directly under the authority of the installation commander.

---

[18] "Threat" is further deconstructed into capability + intent + opportunity.
[19] Engineering Technical Letter (ETL) 11-1, released Mar 2011 by [then] HQ AFCESA/CEO, requires USAF CEs at base level to appoint both primary and alternate IAMs with a focus on certification & accreditation (C&A) of all CE-managed ICS. Note that AFCESA became AFCEC, of AF Civil Engineer Center, in October 2012.
[20] The ICS IAM should be officially designated, trained for the position, and delegated authority to immediately address issues within a defined sphere of responsibility. The ICS IAM should not be an additional-duty position.

2. Form an ICS security team led by the ICS IAM. Securing installation ICS networks cannot be fully accomplished by any single individual or necessarily by any single base entity (such as CEs or PWs typically considered "owners" of the infrastructure). Securing the ICS and reducing risk to mission must be a team effort. This team of authoritative experts should represent at least the CEs/PWs, the cyber unit, physical security, OPSEC, and missions operations. Engineers can inform the "what" and "where"; the cyber or communications experts can provide the "how"; and the mission representatives can explain the "why" as well as the consequences of failure. Intelligence producers can help understand the "who" that represents the threat. The installation commander sets priorities in the form of "when" and makes the critical decisions on commitment and allocation of resources and assets. Include other stakeholders as appropriate to the installation and mission set, such as when there are tenant organizations (e.g., hospital) whose missions may be distinct, but still rely on the installation ICS infrastructure.[21] Consider creating also as a sub-element of this team an ICS-Computer Emergency Response Team (CERT),[22] modeled on that led by Department of Homeland Security (DHS).[23] If a network CERT already resides on the installation, coordinate to include ICS.

3. Direct the ICS security team in identifying existing and/or developing new policies with respect to key elements of the ICS security program.

4. Promulgate policies and concurrently hold training sessions on the policies for all ICS users, operators, and maintainers (analogous: IA training for anyone who touches a network).

5. Implement policies and hold individuals accountable for adherence.

6. Assess effectiveness of measures undertaken (i.e., conduct risk analysis, exercise, red team, or/and tabletop review).

7. Monitor and adjust as needed.

Last resort: An IT IAM could have ICS added to their "job jar" but should receive additional training specific to ICS. Reference also ETL 11-1.

[21] (USAF) SAF/CIO A6, in a Memo dated 20 March 2012 (mandatory compliance) instructed installations to create a multi-disciplined Integrated Product Team (IPT) comprised of all stakeholders to assess IA of PIT, which includes control systems.

[22] CERT = Cyber Emergency Response Team.

[23] The DHS ICS-CERT website is found at http://www.us-cert.gov/control_systems/ics-cert/

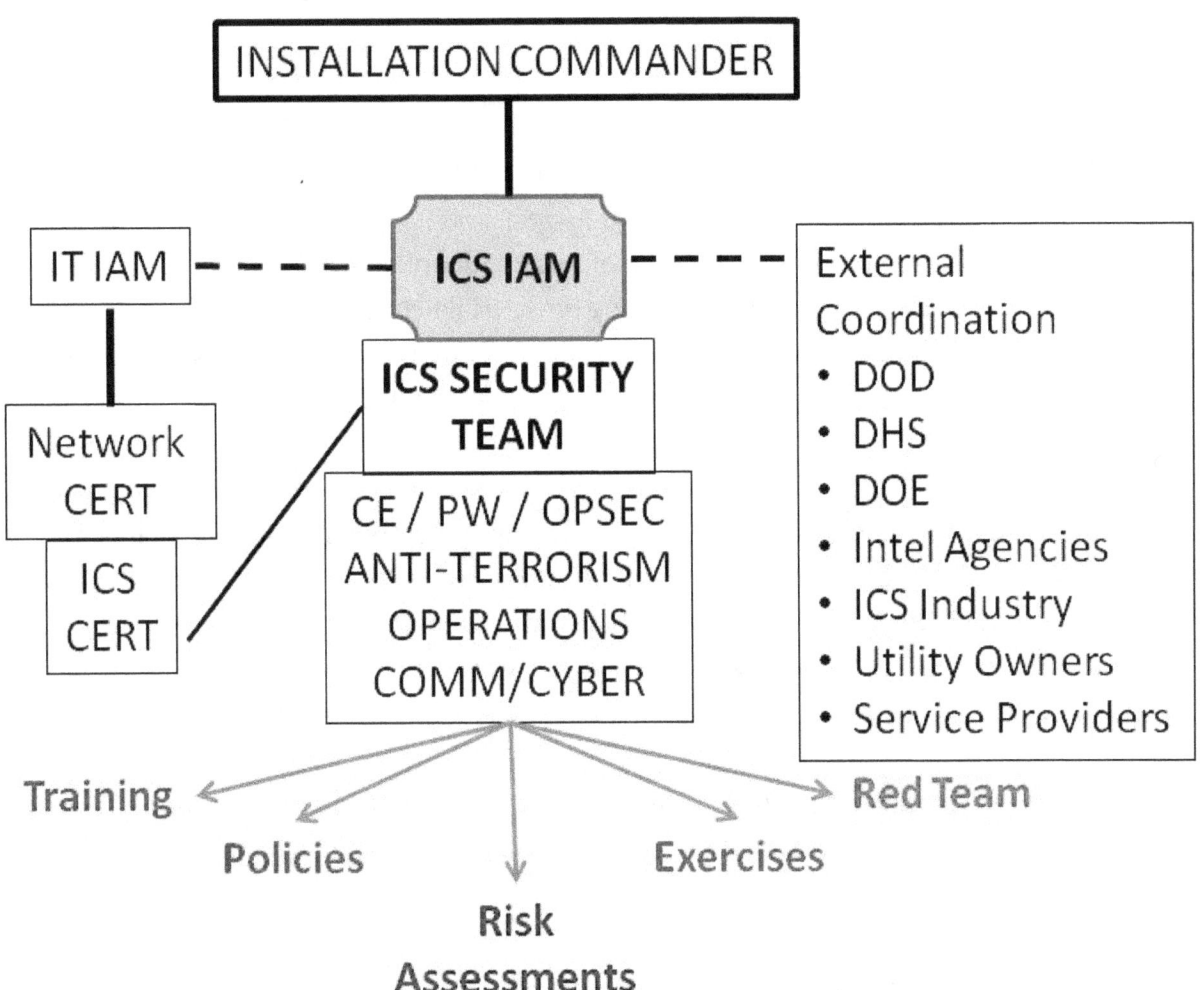

Figure 4. The ICS Security Team

"We also know [enemies] are seeking to create advanced tools to attack [control] systems and cause panic, destruction and even the loss of life."

Secretary of Defense Leon Panetta,
at a meeting in NY City
of Business Executives for National Security (Oct 2012)

Key Point:

- Must begin with missions analysis and prioritization.

The following eight-step process is the heart of this handbook. All other included information is in support of preparing for and understanding the criticality of the assessment process. Best practice is to follow the steps as presented, but individual circumstances may warrant reversing some steps and or accomplishing some in parallel. However approached, <u>Step 1 must always be accomplished first</u>.

While virtually every major entity engaged in ICS defense recommends some version of a "best" process for risk assessment and management, no two approaches are exactly the same. For example OPNAVINST 3500.39C on Operational Risk Management presents a 5-step process.[24] The approach presented here was developed by ICS SMEs working on the National SCADA Test Bed at Idaho National Laboratory (INL) and fits well with a DOD military installation focus.

In association with Step 7 of the process there is also a companion checklist of specific actions to consider. That checklist is found at <u>Attachment 2</u> and is introduced by a textual section titled "<u>Recommended Defense Actions</u>."

Step 1. Mission analysis. For ICS defense, the task is to establish a baseline understanding among the stakeholders of the missions relative to the support infrastructure (both IT and ICS). A key product of this first step is a prioritization of missions that can be linked to assets and then ICS dependencies. <u>Key question</u>: If I have to devote all of my very limited resources to protecting one mission, what would that be? Then the one after that? Applying Mission Assurance Category (MAC) levels[25] can be useful to this endeavor. Also included may be a review of Mission Essential Tasks (MET)[26] with reference to the Defense Readiness Reporting System (DRRS). Mission analysis and decomposition, especially to a granularity useful to the rest of the steps, likely will not be a trivial process and may require significant commitment of the resource of time. A solid investment of time at this step will make the follow-on steps easier to accomplish.

---

[24] The OPNAVINST 5-step ORM process: Identify, Asses, Make decisions, Implement controls and Supervise, remembered by the mnemonic "I AM IS".
[25] MAC definitions found in the *Glossary*.
[26] MET examples in Appendix I.

Step 2. Identify assets. This includes not only direct mission assets (such as aircraft, tanks, ships, etc.) but more pointedly the infrastructure systems (such as fuels management and delivery) that support those. The key is to identify the thread from <u>mission</u> to <u>asset</u> to <u>supporting infrastructure</u> to <u>ICS dependencies</u>. This thread will reveal which ICS systems are more critical when it comes to applying security controls.

> "As a network defender, it is critical to know how the network is laid out as well as the hardware associated with the network. In order to defend SCADA, the operator needs to know what he or she has to work with."
>
> *AFTTP 3-1.CWO (para. 7.6.3.2)*

Step 3. Determine ICS connectivity. It is absolutely essential to identify every point of connectivity because the greatest vulnerability is at any point of connection. While NIPRNet connectivity may take top tier on the list, any connectivity—whether currently connected or *could be* connected later—must be identified. To leave even one *potential* connection undiscovered possibly is to leave the entire network[27] vulnerable. Running a scan on the network elements will identify only what is connected and on at the moment of the scan. This is a key reason for conducting a physical inventory as well, setting eyes on any and every potential connection capability. A PLC may be inside a locked cabinet inside a fenced compound with armed guards at a gate, but if it has an Ethernet port it is <u>connectible</u> (e.g., for vendor maintenance) and therefore, is a potential risk.

Step 4. Determine ICS dependencies. Which missions and their supporting infrastructure are dependent on a properly functioning control system? Are multiple control systems involved (as in the earlier example of traffic control, emergency systems, fuels delivery)? This step also requires technical network mapping typically coupled with a physical inventory and an operational-level understanding of the missions. See <u>Attachment 1</u>, *Mapping Interdependencies*, for an example methodology. A comprehensive approach to this must be followed with collaboration among representatives from at least the cyber, engineering, and mission operations communities.

Step 5. Assess risk. Risk is characterized as an outcome of the interaction among threat, vulnerability, and consequence. The goal is to gain a clear understanding of actual risks that can be managed. All stakeholders need to be engaged in every step of this entire process, but here is where collaboration becomes absolutely essential. Intelligence

---

[27] Arguably extreme, but since we do not know what we do not know (in this example) one is left contemplating "worst case."

analysts help identify external threats; engineer, PWs, and comm/IT specialists provide understanding of the control infrastructure and its vulnerabilities; and operations personnel can define the mission consequences or impacts of a realized threat event. Numerous risk analysis publications and external organizations are available to assist with this step.

Step 6. Prioritize risk management actions. Risk management typically entails deciding among a finite list of response options: avoid, share/transfer, mitigate, or accept. A response option or course of action (COA) typically is selected based on what is feasible, practical, and affordable (i.e., a cost-benefit analysis relative to mission impact). In most cases the commander, decides on a COA and then prioritizes commitment of resources to accomplish the actions.

Step 7. Implement actions. This step requires systematic implementation however simple or complex. At the minimum, one must identify the typical *who* is to do *what*, *where*, and *when*, i.e., direction, responsibility, accountability, and resources available. The *sine qua non* of implementation is <u>commitment</u> of resources combined with accountability mechanisms.

Step 8. Monitor, and reenter the cycle as required. This is never a "fire and forget" activity. Any (even trivial) change to an architecture can introduce new vulnerabilities (emphasizing also the imperative to institute a configuration control process). Additionally, threat actors are continuously on the hunt for vulnerabilities not yet discovered by legitimate owners and operators. To maintain a steady state of security requires continuous monitoring. Furthermore, implementation of any plan is likely to encounter impediments. This will be the phase or step to identify those and readjust as necessary. The success of this step depends on existence of feedback processes and mechanisms, which should have been implemented already.

SOFTWARE TOOLS

Key Point:
- Tools can be good or bad.
- Even a "good" tool is only as good as the expert who uses it.

For many steps in the process of assessing and defending security of ICS, there exists a broad selection of supporting primarily software tools. At the installation command level, it is important simply to note that while such tools are available, tools alone will not guarantee a successful defensive posture of ICS. The human element is essential in every step.

Perhaps **the most important** thing *to understand* about software tools used with or on any ICS is that the tool <u>must not affect the operation of the ICS</u> or, more specifically, the infrastructure it controls. The **most important** thing *to do* with respect to software tools is to defer to IT SMEs who already have a set of approved tools and understand potential impacts of using those tools on particular networks.

Because the services provided by critical infrastructure (electricity heading the list) must always be available, the ICS likewise must be always available. Therefore, any software-based assessment or forensics action upon or through the ICS must not impede, deny, or otherwise alter the system, the data throughput, or the services supported.

Because of the necessity of maintaining availability, due diligence must be exercised if considering use of traditional IT tools (scanners, penetration testers, etc.) on ICS networks. Some IT tools introduce negative effects on the ICS as well as on the controlled infrastructure. Examples are plentiful. The NIST SP 800-82 (p. 3-22) relates one such example:

> "A natural gas utility hired an IT security consulting organization to conduct penetration testing on its corporate IT network. The consulting organization carelessly ventured into a part of the network that was directly connected to the SCADA system. The penetration test locked up the SCADA system and the utility was not able to send gas through its pipelines for four hours. The outcome was the loss of service to its customer base for those four hours."

While significant to those customers, this is trivial compared to impacts on national defense missions. For example, consider potential consequences if the same action involved an ICS supporting fuels management for a combat flying mission or life support systems at a hospital.

ADDITIONAL RESOURCES

Key Point:

- Outside help is available—and much of it is at <u>no cost</u> to the requestor.

Due primarily to the ever-changing nature of the ICS security landscape, published guidance tends to quickly become obsolete. Fortunately, beyond the array of formal publications there exists a helpful offering of additional useful resources. For example:

- Numerous web sites provide detailed information on ICS security issues, current threats, tools, etc. Some of the more prominent are provided as Appendix B, <u>Web Links</u>.
- Students at the Services' advanced Professionally Military Education (PME) schools can be exceptionally good sources for current insights as many engage in fresh research and produce theses specific to emerging ICS/SCADA issues.
- Industry conferences can be exceptional sources of lessons learned and/or best practices, as well as provide opportunity to network with experts.
- Finally, establishing a close relationship with local critical infrastructure owners (e.g., the electric power company, water provider, etc.) can yield better understanding of local threats and risks, and thus better security for the entire community.

For current threat assessment information, sources may include: Air Force Office of Special Investigations (AFOSI), the Army Criminal Investigative Division (CID), or other Service equivalent; intelligence analysts (the J2/A2/G2 shop); and the ICS-CERT's Alerts and Warnings.

ICS SECURITY ACTIONS

Key Point:

- Use this with Step 7 of the <u>Process</u> and with the <u>tabular checklist</u> provided as Attachment 2.

The following section presents a series of action <u>recommendations</u> for securing ICS. Numerous entities, to include DOD, DOE, Commerce Department, and commercial vendors have published similar lists (*see the "<u>References</u>" appendix for some of those*). These recommendations are augmented by the "stand-alone" tabular checklist found at <u>Attachment 2</u>, and most appropriately considered at Step 7 of the "<u>Security Assessment Process</u>."

The recommendations that follow are in an outline that follows the familiar doctrine, organization, training, materiel, leadership & education, personnel, facilities, and policy

DOTMLPF-P[28] framework[29] but with minor modification. The two modifications are that (1) doctrine (D) is not *directly* addressed[30] while (2) cyber security (C) has been added, resulting in a <u>C</u>OTMLPF-P framework that exists only in this publication. "Cyber security" is used here to distinguish between those measures taken in, on and/or through the network(s) and those actions of a more or less physical nature (such as using access control lists). Arguably the most critical set of security measures, cyber security is addressed last because such measures are most effective when supported by solid implementation of actions in the other areas and in particular when guided by clear policy.

RECOMMENDED ICS DEFENSE ACTIONS

POLICY

"The **development of the organization's security policy is the first and most important step in developing an organizational security program**. Security policies lay the groundwork for securing the organization's physical, enterprise, and control system assets." [*Catalog of Control Systems Security*, DHS, Apr 2011, p. 4.] [*emphasis added*]

The National Security Agency (NSA), in its "Securing SCADA and Control Systems" brochure (referring to Sandia National Lab's *Framework for SCADA Security Policy*), states: "A Security Policy defines the controls, behaviors, and expectations of users and processes, and lays the groundwork for securing CS[31] assets. Since the acceptable use of CS is narrower and may have more demanding operational requirements than IT systems, they also **demand their own Security Policy**." [*emphasis added*]

The installation commander must establish authoritative and directive policies with regard to all other aspects of the ICS, thus the rationale for starting with the Policy area.

---

[28] DOTMLPF-P: doctrine, organization, training, materiel, leadership & education, personnel, facilities, and policy. This is borrowed from Chairman Joint Chiefs of Staff Instruction (CJCSI) 3170.01H, Joint Capabilities Integration and Development System (JCIDS); and further acknowledges DoDM 3020.45 Vol 2, Defense Critical Information Program (DCIP) Remediation Planning, which states that remediation planning "shall consider a full range of... [DOTMLPF] options".

[29] Examples of other frameworks: People, processes & technology; strategic, operational & tactical; management, operational & technical.

[30] Any action undertaken in any other area may lead to consideration of doctrinal change. However, this handbook facilitates practical application and so intentionally does not directly address doctrine. Ultimately, best practices may result in recommended changes to doctrine, requiring entering the JCIDS process.

[31] CS = NSA's abbreviation for "control systems."

<u>Policy Actions</u>

- Reuse policy where appropriate. Usually it is not necessary to start from scratch on every policy. Many ICS security issues are also IT and/or IA issues. Many published IT and IA policies may be adapted to ICS. Also, there is increasing promulgation of Service- and DOD-level policies specific to ICS (for example, Air Force Civil Engineering Support Agency[32] [AFCESA]'s ETL 11-1).
- Ensure policies are promulgated to the lowest user level, and require training programs to address ICS policies.
- With the ICS security team (discussed previously), determine which elements of the ICS require specific policies vs. those that may be combined into a single policy document. Examples:
  - An access control policy might include password management, physical facilities control, and connectivity controls.
  - A personnel security policy likely will warrant a dedicated policy document.
- Once complete, the set of policies should address at minimum:
  - Access control
  - Inventory accounting
  - Security of physical assets
  - Configuration control
  - Acquisition of new hardware/software
  - Patching of operating systems and programs
  - Vendor / third-party roles and responsibilities
  - Conduct of vulnerability and risk assessments

LEADERSHIP

Much is subsumed in "leadership." With regard to ICS security it is important that leadership remain engaged and that operators are confident there is a "top-down" emphasis on ICS security. Promulgation of policy is a critical start, but ongoing leadership gives life to those policies. Delegate requisite authority and demand accountability, but do not retreat from oversight.

<u>Leadership Actions</u>

- Conduct periodic awareness briefings to ICS operators and users. Recommend including quarterly reminders of potential threats.

---

[32] In October 2012 AFCESA merged with AFCEE and AFRPA to become AFCEC, or Air Force Civil Engineer Center. ETL 11-1 still validly exists as an AFCESA publication.

- Participate in ICS security stakeholder events, such as DOD conferences, industry group seminars, and on-line discussion forums.
- Establish collaborative relationships with commercial service providers (electric, water, gas, etc.), with focus on their security programs to secure the infrastructure beyond the installation fence. Invite them to training sessions as adjunct members of the security team.
- Identify and mitigate the conditions whereby reliance on vendors creates potential single points of failure. Vendors often are the ones most familiar with installation systems, do not always have immediate access to those systems, and at times can be denied access (such as during elevating FPCONs).
- Add ICS information to the Commander's Critical Information List.
- Engage in the ICS acquisition process from planning through installation; include upgrades to existing systems as well as new systems.
- Develop plans where none exist or otherwise incorporate ICS into those that do. Examples:
  - System Security Plan (SSP)
  - Continuity of Operations Plan (COOP)
  - Disaster Recovery Plan (DRP)
  - Contingency Plans—ICS operation under various INFOCON, FPCON, and other emergencies
  - Operations Security self-assessments and surveys

PERSONNEL

The human element is necessary for the successful operation of ICS, and therefore is a critical area. All individuals who operate, maintain, or otherwise access ICS must understand their respective roles and responsibilities and be appropriately trained to those responsibilities. The insider threat (legitimate operators with legitimate access but illegitimate intent) can overcome most security controls. Even an "honest broker" can make a mistake that results in the same (or worse) impact on mission that a true threat actor can cause.

Personnel Actions
- Ensure every individual is trained for their specific responsibilities and undergoes mandatory periodic update/refresher training (similar to IA training).
- Enforce access controls and establish consequences for violations. For example, every individual has a unique logon (best practice = role-based) and is allowed access only by that logon (i.e., no "guest" accounts).

- Require special background checks on individuals who have access to ICS elements that are critical to mission accomplishment. Consider requiring Secret clearances at least for those individuals with access to mission-critical elements and/or who have full system administration privileges.
- Request ICS managers and operators to sign confidentiality or non-disclosure agreements. Treat ICS information at the very least as unclassified but sensitive.
- Maintain rosters for physical access to facilities, such as rooms where servers are maintained. Require sign-in/sign-out when accessed.
- Create an ICS incident response team modeled on DHS' ICS-CERT.
- Ensure that personnel who resign, retire, or are fired do not have continued access to any element of the ICS. Extend this vigilance to employees of contractors and vendors.
- Ensure that relevant personnel (members of ICS security team, asset owners, etc.) either monitor or routinely are made aware of new vulnerabilities and incidents published by ICS-CERT and ICS component vendors.

TRAINING

Training includes formal, informal, and exercise. Many negative incidents involving ICS, the controlled infrastructure, and/or the missions they support are attributed to legitimate operators who made mistakes due to training deficiencies. A systematic program of mandatory training should be implemented for all managers, operators, and other users of the installation control systems.

Training Actions
- Ensure all operators (at minimum) have had ICS-specific training prior to granting access to any element or component.
- Require IA and OPSEC training for every individual accessing ICS computer systems even if those systems are not directly connected to the IT network. This training must also include contractors and vendors who only sometimes connect to ICS computer systems.
- Provide threat and vulnerability awareness via appropriate forums, unit security awareness training, workplace bulletin boards, etc.
- Exercise plans (incident response, disaster recovery, continuity of operations, etc). Include with other installation exercises where practicable and include ICS-related scenarios under elevating INFOCON and/or FPCON.
- Document all training and ensure each individual maintains currency.

In many cases ICS tend to be "out-of-sight, out-of-mind" to all installation personnel but the CE or PW personnel. As long as the lights are on, water is running, and gates function properly there is no need to be concerned with the systems that make that true. The downside of this view is that it creates a dampening effect on responsibility and accountability for the total ICS infrastructure. While PW/CE accept "ownership" responsibility for the control system field elements, anecdotal information is that the IT side often is viewed as entirely under purview of the IT organization. Conversely, in some cases IT considers the entirety of the ICS network, including the front-end IT elements, as CE's responsibility.[33] The ICS must be considered as a mission-critical system of systems and treated as such organizationally, with collaboration among CE, IT, and the operations' stakeholders. Ill-defined division of labor (responsibility) can create gaps that become threat vectors, or the trade-space of threat actors (both internal and external).

Organization Actions
- Create a position for an ICS IAM with functional authority and direct access to the installation commander. Ensure the IAM's participation in key venues to provide commander advocacy for ICS security and awareness.
- Clarify (and document on command relationship charts) roles and responsibilities of PW/CE, communications, operations (and other stakeholders as appropriate) with respect to operation, maintenance, and security of installation ICS.
- Fully document the ICS—hardware, software, firmware, connectivity, and physical locations of all. Create a topology or ICS system map reflecting connections to supported missions and a logic diagram depicting all information/data flows.
- Assign responsibility for ICS configuration management and control. May require creation of a configuration control board (CCB). The key is this entity documents configuration and maintains continuing control over changes.
- Identify the entity/individuals responsible for developing formal plans (continuity of operations, disaster recovery, etc.).
- Establish roles and responsibilities with regard to third-party relationships.
- Ensure all ICS users and operators understand the chain of command particularly for incident reporting and response mechanisms.

---

[33] On a more positive note, the Air Force has made progress in resolving this issue. Implementation typically lags policy and direction but four key publications have been promulgated beginning in early 2011: SAF/CIO A6 memo of Feb 2011 appointing Designated Accrediting Authority for PIT (includes ICS); SAF/CIO A6 memo (Feb 2011) delegating Certifying Authority to AFCESA/CEO; AFCESA's ETL 11-1 (Mar 2011) which deals with ICS information assurance; and SAF/CIO A6 guidance memo (AFGM2.2, Mar 2012) addressing IA of all PIT and announcing commensurate changes to AFI 33-210.

While some elements of the controlled infrastructure are of necessity exposed (for example the wires of the electric power grid, pipelines for natural gas) most of the control system elements are housed in facilities ranging from guarded buildings to remote access panels. Each type of facility engenders its own relatively unique security challenges, but all share the dichotomous requirement to ensure that legitimate users can gain quick access when necessary while at the same time exclude everyone else from any access whatsoever.

Facilities Actions

- Physically identify and visually inspect every facility that houses any element-of the ICS, however seemingly insignificant. This includes fenced enclosures, buildings, rooms in buildings, field huts, lockboxes, panels, etc. Often overlooked but must be included in "facilities" are the physical connections (e.g., coaxial cable, digital subscriber line (DSL), fiber optics, telephone lines). On large installations it is especially important to identify, inspect, and secure any facility near the perimeter fence (where feasible, relocate away from perimeter).
- Ensure that cabling terminations and their housings are not overlooked. Threats can come from cutting, splicing, tapping, and/or intercepting.
- Develop a plan of action and milestones (POA&M) for addressing physical security deficiencies. An extremely high level of physical security may be achieved by placing cameras, alarms, and armed guards on every facility. However, this typically is neither practical nor cost-efficient. Focus should be on those ICS that are critical to the missions, and then emphasizing where the control system is most exposed to risk. Feasibility, practicality, and expense all will temper selected COAs.
- Create a map of the facilities and the assets housed by each. Use in training, exercises, and actual incident response.
- Ensure portable equipment (e.g., laptops) that may be in storage until required (for backups, recovery, etc.) is included in the inventory and security measures.
- Consider an OPSEC survey focused on ICS. In any event, OPSEC measures should be applied to appropriate elements.

MATERIEL

Consider how physical assets are acquired, maintained, and removed from service. Does policy or other guidance exist? Historically control systems have had a life cycle measured in decades as opposed to IT, which has a life cycle of three years or less. One outcome is that components that have built-in vulnerabilities can remain in the network for years, often without those vulnerabilities and their attendant risks being addressed. Replacement and maintenance of ICS should be approached strategically (i.e., long-term) as well as tactically and operationally.

Materiel Actions

- Assign responsibility for oversight of the physical assets to a configuration control manager or board.
- Establish a formal process for acquisition of new components.
- Operationally test (including vulnerability assessment) proposed new components off-line before introducing into the live network. Collaborate with the National SCADA Test Bed (NSTB) entities (INL, Sandia National Laboratory [SNL]) to test components in "live" and simulated environments.
- Treat adjunct materials (software, tech manuals, SOPs, plans, schematics, etc.) with the same level of security as the ICS.

Cyber security for ICS is in many respects the same as for IT. Most front-end elements (e.g., servers, operating systems, human-machine interfaces, connectivity) are in fact information technology elements. On the other hand, since most non-IT components typically are on a 15-20 year refresh (replacement) cycle and are tied to the operating system with which they originally were installed, even the IT elements can "age-out" or become unsupported making cyber security at the front end more challenging. Differences from IT become more distinct "downstream" in the system, with RTUs, PLCs, and of course the field mechanisms (sensors, gauges, etc.) interfaced directly with the controlled infrastructure. Cyber security applies to all those elements because they are still part of the network. Nearly every component in the system could provide a threat vector into the network. Of primary concern is connectivity from/into NIPRNet and/or any segment of the GIG, but any connection into the system must be considered as creating a risk to the DOD missions of the installation.

> "Asset owners should not assume that their control systems are secure or that they are not operating with an Internet accessible configuration. Instead, asset owners should thoroughly audit their networks for Internet facing devices, weak authentication methods, and component vulnerabilities."
>
> *ICS CERT-ALERT-12-046-01 (Feb 2012)*

This section reflects more actions, and more of them technology-based, than the other (D)OTMLPF-P areas. However, in spite of the expansion of information this listing should not be viewed as absolutely complete, finite, or prescriptive. Existing policies and procedures already in place and proven effective should not be replaced based solely on this listing. Consult other publications (see References), engage the IT and IA professionals, seek assistance/advice from other government-related ICS experts, and consider contracting for assessment services from commercial providers.

Cyber Security Actions

- Define and defend perimeters. "Defense in depth" is an operative phrase often encountered. Strategic approaches include creating enclaves, segmentation, and establishing demilitarized zones (DMZ), typically using firewalls. NSA, DHS, and others recommend total isolation of ICS networks but that is not always possible or practical. Where some connectivity is required, at least secure the points where connection can be made.
- Control web access. Where Internet or NIPRNet connectivity is required limit access to the web by turning off unnecessary web services and ports, and consider using "white" and/or

"black" lists of allowed/not allowed sites. (Note: Whitelisting is often preferred over blacklisting.)

- Protect data. Encrypt mission-critical data in transmission and provide backups or other redundancies for data in stasis (files, databases, etc.). As a caveat, downstream data such as between a PLC and a field device <u>cannot</u> be encrypted.

- Protect the operating system. Perimeter defense is a good start, but threat actors (insiders, for example) can find ways inside the perimeter. Use defensive tools[34] (software) such as for intrusion detection. Implement and update virus-checking software (may need to do manually if not connected). Establish a patching protocol (typically requires testing off-line first). Enable audit logging, and review the logs frequently to detect anomalous (especially illegitimate) activity. Also, remove all services, programs, etc. not needed for operation of the ICS.

- Manage installation of new assets. Ensure hardware and software factory default or contractor-enabled settings are changed. Do not allow anything that is connected/connectable, new or legacy, to be accessed using default passwords. Vendors prefer to maintain defaults especially on field devices (e.g., PLCs) for ease of maintenance access. Those same defaults typically are publically accessible, often published on vendor company web sites, and <u>will</u> be used by threat actors.

- Disable every connection point not needed. Points include USB ports, wireless access points, Ethernet jacks, satellite receivers, modems, etc. Provide positive control over all remaining points, ensuring no "backdoor" exists. Even one unguarded USB port can provide a devastating threat vector. This point is demonstrated by the publically reported outcome of the Stuxnet infection of an Iranian nuclear processing facility's centrifuge control system.

- Control individual access to all elements. The operating system server and workstations are obvious control points but some field elements such as PLCs can (and do) have separate logons. There are a number of operational and tactical actions to take, selectively or collectively. Foremost is to require each individual to have a unique (unshared) logon ID and password.[35] Policy should strictly prohibit shared passwords. Institute least-privilege and role-based access. Absolutely nothing should be accessible via "guest" or anonymous accounts, in spite of very plausible rationale for such given by vendors. Administrator privileges should be given to vendors only as required and then closely monitored.

---

[34] Discussed elsewhere, but a reminder is warranted: Be cautious with software tools. Some very effective tools for IT networks can cause problems on ICS. Typically, passivity is the key characteristic. Tools that interact with the system, such as for intrusion protection mostly, are to be avoided. If an interactive tools is determined to be necessary it must first be tested off-line before use on ICS. Even if it "passes" the test, tools should be closely monitored for unanticipated, undiscovered negative effects.

[35] Air Force is implementing Public Key Infrastructure (PKI) as widely as possible. Also, DoD-wide many logons are accomplished with a Common Access Card (CAC). Aside from the method of network access, the key takeaway is unique, linked to a vetted user, not shareable with anyone else.

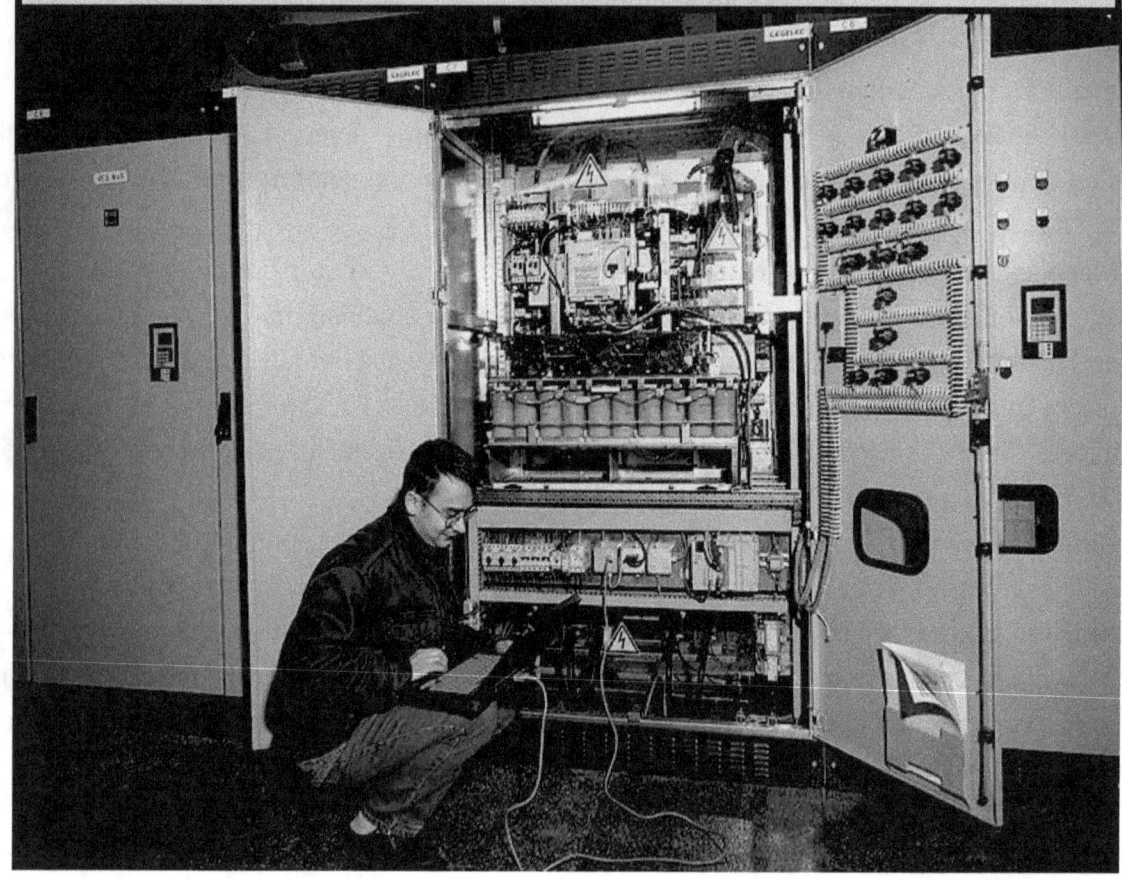

Figure 5. It Only Takes a Minute

APPENDIX A   REFERENCES

262 NWS, *Assessment of ICS Safe Harbor on Altus AFB*, 2010.

AFI 10-710, *Information Operations Condition (INFOCON)*, 2006.

AFI 32-1063, *Electric Power Systems*, 2005 [certified current 2010].

AFI 33-112, *Information Technology Hardware Asset Management*, 2011.

AFI 33-200, *Information Assurance Management*, 2008 [change 2, 2010].

AFI 33-210, *Air Force Certification and Accreditation Program*, [with attached SAF/CIO A6 guidance memo, AFGM 2.2, 2012, on the AFCAP] 2008.

AFMAN 33-282, *Computer Security (COMPUSEC)*, 2012.

AFNIC, EV 2010-08, *Guide for Submission of Platform Information Technology (PIT) Determination Concurrence Requests*, 2010.

AFPD 10-24, *Air Force Critical Infrastructure Program (CIP)*, 2006.

AFPD 32-10, *Installations and Facilities*, 2010.

AFPD 33-2, *Information Assurance (IA) Program*, 2007.

AR 25-2, *Information Assurance*, (Revised) 2009.

CJCSI 3209.01, *Defense Critical Infrastructure Program,* 2012.

CJCSI 6510.01F, *Information Assurance and Support to CND*, 2011.

CJCSM 6510.01, *Defense-in-Depth: Information Assurance (IA) and Computer Network Defense (CND)*, 2006.

CNSSI 1253, *Security Categorization and Control Selection for National Security Systems*, 2012.

CNSSI 4009, *National Information Assurance (IA) Glossary*, 2010.

CNSSP 22, *Policy on Information Assurance Risk Management for National Security Systems*, 2012.

DHS, *Catalog of Control Systems Security: Recommendations for Standards Developers*, 2011.

DHS, *Cross-Sector Roadmap for Cybersecurity of Control Systems*, 2011.

DHS, *Common Cybersecurity Vulnerabilities in ICS*, 2011.

DHS, *Cyber Security Assessments of Industrial Control Systems*, 2010.

DHS, *Cyber Security Procurement Language for Control Systems*, 2009.

DHS, *Primer: Control Systems Cyber Security Framework and Technical Metrics*, 2009.

DHS, *Recommended Practice: Creating Cyber Forensics Plans for Control Systems*, 2008.

DHS, *Recommended Practice: Developing an ICS Cybersecurity Incident Response Capability*, 2009.

DHS, *Improving Industrial Control Systems Cybersecurity with Defense-In-Depth Strategies*, 2009.

DHS, *Recommended Practices for Securing Control System Modems*, 2008.

DHS, *Risk Lexicon*, 2010.

DISA, *DOD Internet-NIPRNet DMZ Increment 1, Phase 1: Technology Overview*, 2011.

DISA, *Enclave Security Technical Implementation Guide* (STIG), 2011.

DOD, *Risk Management Guide for DOD Acquisition, Sixth Edition*, 2006.

DODD 3020.26, *Department of Defense Continuity Programs*, 2009.

DODD 3020.40, *DOD Policy and Responsibilities for Critical Infrastructure*, 2010.

DODD 5205.02E, *DoD Operations Security (OPSEC) Program*, 2012.

DODD 8100.02, *Use of Commercial Wireless Devices, Services, and Technologies in the Department of Defense (DOD) Global Information Grid (GIG)*, 2004 [certified current as of 2007].

DODD 8500.01E, *Information Assurance*, 2007.

DODD 8570.01, *Information Assurance Training, Certification, and Workforce Management*, 2004 [certified current as of 2007].

DODI 2000.12, *DOD Antiterrorism (AT) Program*, 2012.

DODI 3020.45, *Defense Critical Infrastructure Program (DCIP) Management*, 2008.

DODI 4170.11, *Installation Energy Management*, 2009.

DODI 5205.13, *Defense Industrial Base Cyber Security/Information Assurance*, 2010.

DODI 5240.19, *Counterintelligence Support to the Defense Critical Infrastructure Program*, 2007.

DODI 6055.17, *DOD Installation Emergency Management (IEM) Program*, 2010.

DODI 8500.2, *Information Assurance (IA) Implementation*, 2003.

DODI 8510.01, *Department of Defense Information Assurance Certification and Accreditation Process (DIACAP)*, 2007.

DODI 8551.1, *Ports, Protocols, and Services Management (PPSM)*, 2004.

DODI 8582.01, *Security of Unclassified DOD Information on Non-DOD Information Systems*, 2012.

DODM 3020.45, Vol. 1, *Defense Critical Infrastructure Program (DCIP): DOD Mission-Based Critical Asset Identification Process (CAIP)*, 2008.

DODM 5205.02-M, *DoD Operations Security (OPSEC) Program Manual*, 2008.

DOE, *21 Steps to Improve Cyber Security of SCADA Networks*, 2002.

DOE, *Electricity Sector Subsector Risk Management Process (draft for public comment)*, 2012.

DOE / PNNL-20376, *Secure Data Transfer Guidance for Industrial Control and SCADA Systems*, 2011.

DON (Dept. of the Navy), *CIO Memo 02-10, Information Assurance Policy Update for Platform Information Technology*, 2010.

ETL 11-1, [USAF] *Civil Engineer ICS Information Assurance Compliance*, 2011.

FIPS 199, *Standards for Security Categorization of Federal Information and Information Systems*, 2004.

FIPS 200, *Minimum Security Requirements for Federal Information and Information Systems*, 2006.

HSPD 7, *Critical Infrastructure Identification, Prioritization, and Protection*, 2003.

IEEE C37.1, *IEEE Standard for SCADA and Automation Systems*, 2008.

INL/EXT-07-12635, *Recommended Practice for Securing Control System Modems*, 2008.

INL/EXT-08-13979, *Common Cyber Security Vulnerabilities Observed in Control System Assessments by the INL NSTB Program*, 2008.

INL/EXT-10-18381, *NSTB Assessments Summary Report: Common Industrial Control System Cyber Security Weaknesses*, 2010. (Reissued in 2011 as *Vulnerability Analysis of Energy Delivery Control Systems.)*

ISO 31000, *Risk Management–Principles and Guidelines*, 2009.

ITL Bulletin 8/11, *Protecting ICS–Key Components of Our Nation's Critical Infrastructures*, 2011.

JP 3-27, *Homeland Defense*, 2007.

JTF CapMed Inst. 8510.01, *Information Technology (IT) Platform Guide*, 2011.

MCO 3501.36A, *Marine Corps Critical Infrastructure Program (MCCIP)*, 2008.

NERC CIPs 002-009, *Critical Infrastructure Protection Series.* (Version 4 released 2012; version 5 in review process.)

NIST Interagency Report 7435, *The Common Vulnerability Scoring System (CVSS) and Its Applicability to Federal Agency Systems*, 2007.

NIST SP 800-30, Rev. 1, *Guide for Conducting Risk Assessments*, 2011.

NIST SP 800-37, Rev. 1, *Guide for Applying the Risk Management Framework to Federal Information Systems: A Security Life Cycle Approach*, 2010.

NIST SP 800-39, *Managing Information Security Risk*, 2011.

NIST SP 800-40, V.2, *Creating a Patch and Vulnerability Management Program*, 2005.

NIST SP 800-41, Rev. 1, *Guidelines on Firewalls and Firewall Policy*, 2009.

NIST SP 800-53, Rev. 4, *Security & Privacy Controls for Federal Information Systems and Organizations*, 2012.

NIST SP 800-53A, Rev. 1, *Guide for Assessing the Security Controls in Federal Information Systems and Organizations: Building Effective Security Assessment Plans*, 2010.

NIST SP 800-61, Rev. 2, *Computer Security Incident Handling Guide (Draft)*, 2012.

NIST SP 800-82, *Guide to Industrial Control Systems Security*, 2011.

NIST SP 800-92, *Guide to Computer Security Log Management*, 2006.

NIST SP 800-94, *Guide to Intrusion Detection and Prevention Systems*, 2007.

NSA, *A Framework for Assessing and Improving the Security Posture of Industrial Control Systems,* 2010.

NSTB, *NSTB Assessments Summary Report: Common Industrial Control System Cyber Security Weaknesses*, 2010.

SECNAVINST 3501.1B, *Department of the Navy Critical Infrastructure Protection Program*, 2010.

SECNAVINST 5239.3A, *Department of the Navy Information Assurance (IA) Policy*, 2004.

SNL, Sandia Report SAND2004-4233, *A Classification Scheme for Risk Assessment Methods*, 2004.

SNL, Sandia Report SAND2007-2070P, *Security Metrics for Process Control Systems*, 2007.

SNL, Sandia Report SAND2010-5183, *Control System Devices: Architectures and Supply Channels Overview*, 2011.

US Army TM 5-601, *SCADA Systems for C4ISR Facilities*, 2006.

262 NWS	http://washingtonairguard.org/194rsw/
346 TS [CAC required]	https://www.my.af.mil/gcss-af/USAF/ep/globalTab.do?channelPageId=sF575FC8E22DC74AF01230B02FDC91C2B
AFCESA	http://www.afcesa.af.mil/ *Note that AFCESA became AFCEC in October 2012.*
CSET (DHS)	http://www.us-cert.gov/control_systems/satool.html
DTIC	http://www.dtic.mil/dtic/
DUSD (I&E)	http://www.acq.osd.mil/ie/
DOE / Energy.gov	http://energy.gov/oe/downloads/roadmap-achieve-energy-delivery-systems-cybersecurity-2011 "Roadmap to Achieve Energy Delivery Systems Cybersecurity"
DOE / Energy.gov	http://energy.gov/oe/services/cybersecurity/cybersecurity-risk-management-process-rmp Cybersecurity Risk Management process
ICS-CERT (DHS)	http://www.us-cert.gov/control_systems/ics-cert/
ICS-CERT	http://www.us-cert.gov/control_systems/cstraining.html Control Systems Security Program (CSSP) Training opportunities
Idaho NL	https://inlportal.inl.gov/portal/server.pt/community/home/255
Interagency OPSEC Support Staff (IOSS)	http://www.ioss.gov *[requires DoD credentials, e.g., CAC, to access]*
JDEIS	https://jdeis.js.mil/jdeis/index.jsp?pindex=0 links to DOD and CJCS issuances
NIST	http://www.nist.gov/index.html
Pacific Northwest NL	http://www.pnnl.gov/
Sandia NL	http://www.sandia.gov/ http://energy.sandia.gov/?page_id=5800
SCADA Test Bed	http://www.inl.gov/scada/
USACE	http://www.usace.army.mil/
Vulnerability Database	http://nvd.nist.gov/

APPENDIX C   ACRONYMS

AFCEC	Air Force Civil Engineer Command [result of Oct 2012 merger of AFCESA, AFCEE and AFRPA]
AFCESA	Air Force Civil Engineer Support Agency [later AFCEC]
AFI	Air Force Instruction
AFMAN	Air Force Manual
AFNIC	Air Force Network Integration Center
AFOSI	Air Force Office of Special Investigations
AFPD	Air Force policy Directive
AFTTP	Air Force Tactics, Techniques, and Procedures
AIC	availability, integrity, confidentiality [vs. IT systems' CIA]
AIS	automated information system
AMI	Advanced Metering Infrastructure
APT	Advanced Persistent Threat
AR	Army Regulation
AT	antiterrorism
AV	antivirus
CAC	common access card
CAIP	critical asset identification process
C&A	certification & accreditation
CCB	Configuration Control Board
CCDR	combatant commander
CE	civil engineer
CERT	Computer Emergency Readiness Team
CIA	confidentiality, integrity, availability [vs. ICS systems' AIC]
CID	Criminal Investigation Division
CJCSI	Chairman, Joint Chiefs of Staff Instruction
CJCSM	Chairman, Joint Chiefs of Staff Manual
CNSS	Committee on National Security Systems
CNSSI	Committee on National Security Systems Instruction
CNSSP	Committee on National Security Systems Pamphlet
COA	course of action
COOP	Continuity of Operations Plan
COTS	commercial off-the-shelf
CPNI	Center for the Protection of National Infrastructure
CS	control system [NSA term]
CSET	Cyber Security Evaluation Tool

CVSS	Common Vulnerability Scoring System
DCI	Defense Critical Infrastructure
DCIP	Defense Critical Infrastructure Program
DCS	Distributed Control System
DEP	data execution prevention
DHS	Department of Homeland Security
DIACAP	DoD Information Assurance Certification & Accreditation Process
DISA	Defense Information Systems Agency
DSL	digital subscriber line
DISLA	Defense Infrastructure Sector Lead Agent
DMZ	demilitarized zone
DOD	Department of Defense
DODD	Department of Defense Directive
DODI	Department of Defense Instruction
DODM	Department of Defense Manual
DOE	Department of Energy
DON	Department of the Navy
DOTMLPF-P	Doctrine, Organization, Training, Materiel, Leadership (& education), Personnel, Facilities, and Policy
DRP	Disaster Recovery Plan
DRRS	Defense Readiness Reporting System
DTIC	Defense Technical Information Center
DUSD	Deputy Under Secretary of Defense
EMCS	Energy Management Control System
EMS	Emergency Medical Services
ETL	Engineering Technical Letter
FIPS	Federal Information Processing Standards
FPCON	Force Protection Condition
GAO	Government Accountability Office
GIG	Global Information Grid
GIS	geographical information services
HIPS	McAfee Host Intrusion Prevention System
HSPD	Homeland Security Presidential Directive
HVAC	Heating, Ventilation and Air Conditioning
IA	information assurance
IAM	Information Assurance Manager
ICS	Industrial Control Systems [*US Army has used ICS also for "Instrumentation Communication Subsystem"*]

ICS-CERT	ICS Cyber Emergency Response Team
IDART	Information Design Assurance Red Team
IDS	intrusion detection system
IEEE	Institute of Electrical and Electronics Engineers
IEM	Installation Emergency Management
INFOCON	Information Operations Condition
INL	Idaho National Laboratory
IPS	intrusion prevention system
IPT	Integrated Product Team
IS	information system
ISO	International Organization for Standardization
ISP	Internet service provider
ISSM	Information System Security Manager
IT	information technology
JCIDS	Joint Capabilities Integration and Development System
JDEIS	Joint Doctrine, Education, and Training Electronic Information System
JIT	just in time *[refers to a just-in-time compiler]*
JP	Joint Publication
JTF	Joint Task Force
JWAG	Joint Warfighter Advisory Group
LUA	least user access
MAC	Mission Assurance Category
MCCIP	Marine Corps Critical Infrastructure Program
MCO	Marine Corps Order
MEF	mission essential functions
MET	mission essential task
MMS	multimedia messaging service
NERC CIPS	North American Electric Reliability Council Critical Infrastructure Protection Series
NIPRNet	Non-secure Internet Protocol Router Network
NIST	National Institute of Standards and Technology
NSA	National Security Agency
NSTB	National SCADA Test Bed
OPNAVINST	Office of the Chief of Naval Operations Instruction
OPSEC	operations security
OSI	open system interconnect
OT	operational technology
PIT	Platform Information Technology (*includes ICS*)

PIT-I	PIT Interconnect [*refers to PIT connected to IT network*]
PKI	Public Key Infrastructure
PLC	Programmable Logic Controller
PME	Professional Military Education
PNNL	Pacific Northwest National Laboratory
POA&M	Plan of Actions & Milestones
PW	public works
RBAC	role-based access control
ROP	return-oriented programming
RTU	Remote Terminal Unit
SCADA	Supervisory Control and Data Acquisition
SECNAVINST	Secretary of the Navy Instruction
SMB	server message block
SME	subject matter expert
SMS	short message service
SNL	Sandia National Laboratory
SOP	standard operating procedures
SP	Special Publication
SSP	System Security Plan
STIG	Security Technical Implementation Guide
TM	Technical Manual
UAC	user access control
USACE	United States Army Corps of Engineers
USB	Universal Serial Bus
USSTRATCOM	United States Strategic Command
VoIP	voice over Internet Protocol
VPN	virtual private network
WAF	web application firewall

Advanced Persistent Threat. An adversary that possesses sophisticated levels of expertise and significant resources, which allow it to create opportunities to achieve its objectives by using multiple attack vectors (e.g., cyber, physical, and deception). These objectives typically include establishing and extending footholds within the information technology infrastructure of the targeted organizations for purposes of exfiltrating information, undermining or impeding critical aspects of a mission, program, or organization; or positioning itself to carry out these objectives in the future. The advanced persistent threat: (i) pursues its objectives repeatedly over an extended period of time; (ii) adapts to defenders' efforts to resist it; and (iii) is determined to maintain the level of interaction needed to execute its objectives. [NIST SP 800-53 Rev 4]

- Advanced: The actor is adaptive and able to evade detection and is able to gain and maintain access to protected networks and resident sensitive information.
- Persistent: The actor has a strong foothold in/on the target network and is exceptionally difficult to completely remove or deny even if detected.
- Threat: The actor has both capability and intent that is counter to the best interests of the network and/or the legitimate users.

Asset. A distinguishable entity that provides a service or capability. Assets are people, physical entities, or information located either within or outside the United States and employed, owned, or operated by domestic, foreign, public, or private sector organizations. [DODD 3020.40]

Configuration Control. Process for controlling modifications to hardware, firmware, software, and documentation to protect the information system against improper modifications before, during, and after system implementation. [NIST SP 800-53]

Defense Critical Infrastructure (DCI). DCI is the DOD and non-DOD networked assets essential to project, support, and sustain military forces and operations worldwide. Assets are people, physical entities, or information. Physical assets would include installations, facilities, ports, bridges, power stations, telecommunication lines, pipelines, etc. The increasing interconnectivity and interdependence among commercial and defense infrastructures demand that DOD take steps to understand and remedy or mitigate the vulnerabilities of, and threats to, the critical infrastructures on which it depends for mission accomplishment. The DCIP is a fully integrated program that provides a comprehensive process for understanding and protecting selected infrastructure assets that are critical to national security during peace, crisis, and war. It involves identifying, prioritizing, assessing, protecting, monitoring, and assuring the reliability and availability of mission-critical infrastructures essential to the execution of the NMS. The program also addresses the operational decision support necessary for CCDRs to achieve their mission objectives despite the degradation or absence of these infrastructures. [**Joint Publication 3-27**] [*see also*: DODD 3020.40, DODI 3020.45, and DODM 2020.45 vols 1-5]

Defense-in-Depth. Information security strategy integrating people, technology, and operations capabilities to establish variable barriers across multiple layers and missions of the organization. [NIST SP 800-39]

Disaster Recovery Plan (DRP). A written plan for processing critical applications in the event of a major hardware or software failure or destruction of facilities. [NIST SP 800-82]

DOD Information Assurance Certification and Accreditation Process (DIACAP). The DOD process for identifying, implementing, validating, certifying, and managing IA capabilities and services, expressed as IA controls, and authorizing the operation of DOD ISs, including testing in a live environment, in accordance with statutory, Federal, and DOD requirements. [DODI 8510.01]

Enclave. Collection of computing environments connected by one or more internal networks under the control of a single authority and security policy, including personnel and physical security. Enclaves always assume the highest mission assurance category and security classification of the AIS applications or outsourced IT-based processes they support, and derive their security needs from those systems. They provide standard IA capabilities such as boundary defense, incident detection and response, and key management, and also deliver common applications such as office automation and electronic mail...Enclaves may be specific to an organization or a mission, and the computing environments may be organized by physical proximity or by function independent of location. Examples of enclaves include local area networks and the applications they host, backbone networks, and data processing centers. [DODD 8500.01E]

Force Protection Condition (FPCON). A Chairman of the Joint Chiefs of Staff-approved standard for identification of and recommended responses to terrorist threats against US personnel and facilities. [Joint Pub 1-02]

Incident. An occurrence that actually or potentially jeopardizes the confidentiality, integrity, or availability of an information system or the information the system processes, stores, or transmits or that constitutes a violation or imminent threat of violation of security policies, security procedures, or acceptable use policies. Incidents may be intentional or unintentional. [NIST SP 800-82]

Information Assurance (IA). Measures that protect and defend information and information systems by ensuring their availability, integrity, authentication, confidentiality, and non-repudiation. This includes providing for restoration of information systems by incorporating protection, detection, and reaction capabilities. [DODD 8500.01E]

Information Assurance Manager (IAM). The individual responsible for the information assurance program of a DOD information system or organization. While the term IAM is favored within the Department of Defense, it may be used interchangeably with the IA title Information Systems Security Manager (ISSM). [DODI 8500.2]

Information Operations Condition (INFOCON). The INFOCON system provides a framework within which the Commander USSTRATCOM (CDRUSSTRATCOM), regional commanders, service chiefs, base/post/camp/station/vessel commanders, or agency directors can increase the measurable readiness of their networks to match operational priorities. [CJCSI 6510.01F]

Intrusion Detection System (IDS). A security service that monitors and analyzes network or system events for the purpose of finding, and providing real-time or near real-time warning of, attempts to access system resources in an unauthorized manner. [NIST SP 800-82]

Intrusion Prevention System (IPS). A system that can detect an intrusive activity and can also attempt to stop the activity, ideally before it reaches its targets. [NIST SP 800-82]

Mission Assurance. A process to ensure that assigned tasks or duties can be performed in accordance with the intended purpose or plan. It is a summation of the activities and measures taken to ensure that required capabilities and all supporting infrastructures are available to the Department of Defense to carry out the National Military Strategy. It links numerous risk management program activities and security-related functions, such as force protection; antiterrorism; critical infrastructure protection; IA; continuity of operations; chemical, biological, radiological, nuclear, and high explosive defense; readiness; and installation preparedness to create the synergy required for the Department of Defense to mobilize, deploy, support, and sustain military operations throughout the continuum of operations. [DODD 3020.40]

Mission Assurance Category (MAC). Applicable to DOD information systems, the mission assurance category reflects the importance of information relative to the achievement of DOD goals and objectives, particularly the warfighters' combat mission. Mission assurance categories are primarily used to determine the requirements for availability and integrity. The Department of Defense has three defined mission assurance categories: [DODD 8500.01E]

- MAC I. Systems handling information that is determined to be vital to the operational readiness or mission effectiveness of deployed and contingency forces in terms of both content and timeliness. The consequences of loss of integrity or availability of a MAC I system are unacceptable and could include the immediate and sustained loss of mission effectiveness. MAC I systems require the most stringent protection measures.

- MAC II. Systems handling information that is important to the support of deployed and contingency forces. The consequences of loss of integrity are unacceptable. Loss of availability is difficult to deal with and can only be tolerated for a short time. The consequences could include delay or degradation in providing important support services or commodities that may seriously impact mission effectiveness or operational readiness. MAC II systems require additional safeguards beyond best practices to ensure adequate assurance.

- MAC III. Systems handling information that is necessary for the conduct of day-to-day business, but does not materially affect support to deployed or contingency forces in the short-term. The consequences of loss of integrity or availability can be tolerated or overcome without significant impacts on mission effectiveness or operational readiness. The consequences could include the delay or degradation of services or commodities enabling routine activities. MAC III systems require protective measures, techniques, or procedures generally commensurate with commercial best practices.

Mission Essential Functions (MEF). The specified or implied tasks required to be performed by, or derived from, statute, Executive Order, or other appropriate guidance, and those organizational activities that must be performed under all circumstances to achieve DOD component missions or responsibilities in a continuity threat or event. Failure to perform or sustain these functions would significantly affect the Department of Defense's ability to provide vital services or exercise authority, direction, and control. [DODD 3020.26]

National Security System. Any information system (including any telecommunications system) used or operated by an agency or by a contractor of an agency, or other organization on behalf of an agency—(i) the function, operation, or use of which involves intelligence activities; involves cryptologic activities related to national security; involves command and control of military forces; involves equipment that is an integral part of a weapon or weapons system; or is critical to the direct fulfillment of military or intelligence missions (excluding a system that is to be used for routine administrative and business applications, for example, payroll, finance, logistics, and personnel management applications); or (ii) is protected at all times by procedures established for information that have been specifically authorized under criteria established by an Executive Order or an Act of Congress to be kept classified in the interest of national defense or foreign policy. [44 U.S.C., Sec. 3542]

Platform Information Technology (PIT) and PIT-Interconnection (PITI). For DOD IA purposes, platform IT interconnection refers to network access to platform IT. Platform IT interconnection has readily identifiable security considerations and needs that must be addressed in both acquisition, and operations. Platform IT refers to computer resources, both hardware and software, that are physically part of, dedicated to, or **essential in real time to the mission performance of special purpose systems** such as weapons, training simulators, diagnostic test and maintenance equipment, calibration equipment, equipment used in the research and development of weapons systems, medical technologies, transport vehicles, **buildings**, and **utility distribution systems** such as water and electric. Examples of platform IT interconnections that impose security considerations include communications interfaces for data exchanges with enclaves for mission planning or execution, remote administration, and remote upgrade or reconfiguration. [*emphasis added*] [DODD 8500.01E, DODI 8500.2]

Risk.

- Potential for an unwanted outcome resulting from an incident, event, or occurrence, as determined by its likelihood and the associated consequences. [DHS Risk Lexicon]
- A measure of the extent to which an entity is threatened by a potential circumstance or event, and typically a function of: (i) the adverse impacts that would arise if the circumstance or event occurs; and (ii) the likelihood of occurrence. [CNSSI 4009]
- An expression of consequences in terms of the probability of an event occurring, the severity of the event and the exposure of personnel or resources to potential loss or harm. A general expression of risk as a function of probability [P], severity [S], and exposure [E] can be written as: Risk = f(P, S, E). [AFPAM 90-902]

Risk Assessment. The process of identifying risks to organizational operations (including mission, functions, image, reputation), organizational assets, individuals, other organizations, and the Nation, resulting from the operation of an information system. Part of risk management, incorporates threat and vulnerability analyses, and considers mitigations provided by security controls planned or in place. Synonymous with risk analysis. [NIST SP 800-53]

Risk Management. The program and supporting processes to manage information security risk to organizational operations (including mission, functions, image, reputation), organizational assets, individuals, other organizations, and the Nation, and includes: (i) establishing the context for risk-related activities; (ii) assessing risk; (iii) responding to risk once determined; and (iv) monitoring risk over time. [NIST SP 800-53]

Risk Management Strategies. [DHS Risk Lexicon]
- Acceptance: explicit or implicit decision not to take an action that would affect all or part of a particular risk.
- Avoidance: strategies or measures taken that effectively remove exposure to a risk.
- Mitigation: application of measure or measures to reduce the likelihood of an unwanted occurrence and/or its consequences.
- Transfer: action taken to manage risk that shifts some or all of the risk to another entity, asset, system, network, or geographic area.

Risk Mitigation. Prioritizing, evaluating, and implementing the appropriate risk-reducing controls/countermeasures recommended from the risk management process. [NIST SP 800-53]

Security Audit. Independent review and examination of a system's records and activities to determine the adequacy of system controls, ensure compliance with established security policy and procedures, detect breaches in security services, and recommend any changes that are indicated for countermeasures. [NIST SP 800-82]

Security Policy. Security policies define the objectives and constraints for the security program. Policies are created at several levels, ranging from organization or corporate policy to specific operational constraints (e.g., remote access). In general, policies provide answers to the questions "what" and "why" without dealing with "how." Policies are normally stated in terms that are technology-independent. [NIST SP 800-82]

System Security Plan (SSP). Formal document that provides an overview of the security requirements for an information system and describes the security controls in place or planned for meeting those requirements. [NIST SP 800-18]

Supervisory Control and Data Acquisition (SCADA). A generic name for a computerized system that is capable of gathering and processing data and applying operational controls over long distances. Typical uses include power transmission and distribution and pipeline systems. SCADA was designed for the unique communication challenges (e.g., delays, data integrity) posed by the various media that must be used, such as phone lines, microwave, and satellite. Usually shared rather than dedicated. [NIST SP 800-82]

Task Critical Asset. An asset that is of such extraordinary importance that its incapacitation or destruction would have a serious, debilitating effect on the ability of one or more DOD Components or DISLA organizations to execute the task or mission-essential task it supports. Task critical assets are used to identify defense critical assets. [DODD 3020.40]

Virtual Private Network (VPN). A restricted-use, logical (i.e., artificial or simulated) computer network that is constructed from the system resources of a relatively public, physical (i.e., real) network (such as the Internet), often by using encryption (located at hosts or gateways), and often by tunneling links of the virtual network across the real network. [NIST SP 800-82]

Vulnerability Assessment. Systematic examination of an information system or product to determine the adequacy of security measures, identify security deficiencies, provide data from which to predict the effectiveness of proposed security measures, and confirm the adequacy of such measures after implementation. [NIST SP 800-39]

APPENDIX E   CE BRIEFING GRAPHICS

The following two graphics were extracted from an AFCESA brief dated February 2012. (*The Reference Model is modified from the original*.) They are offered simply as representative of a Service view of ICS.

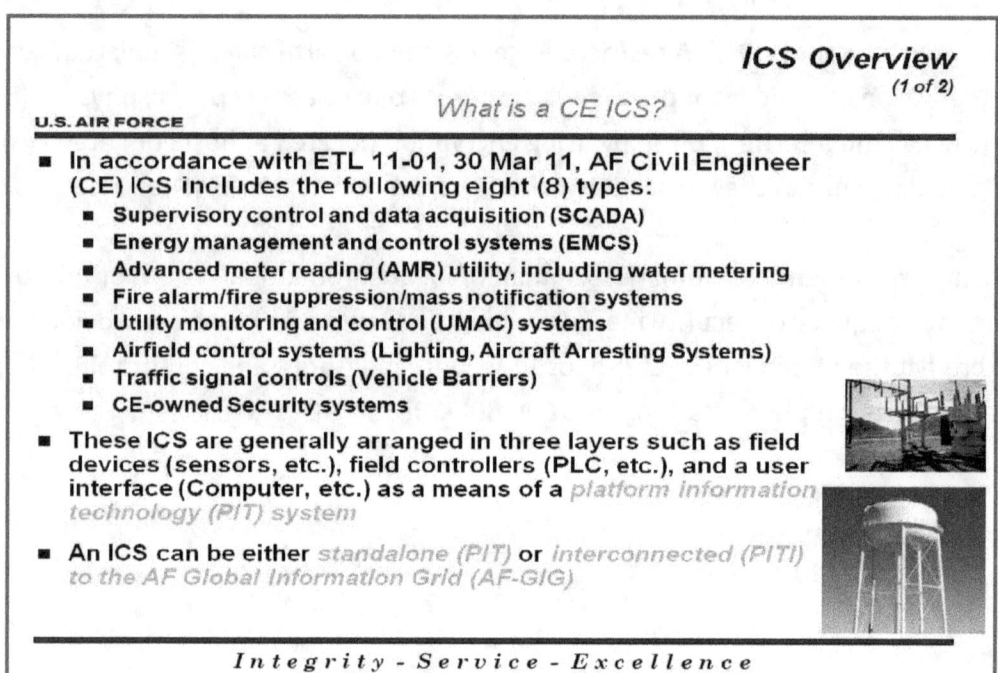

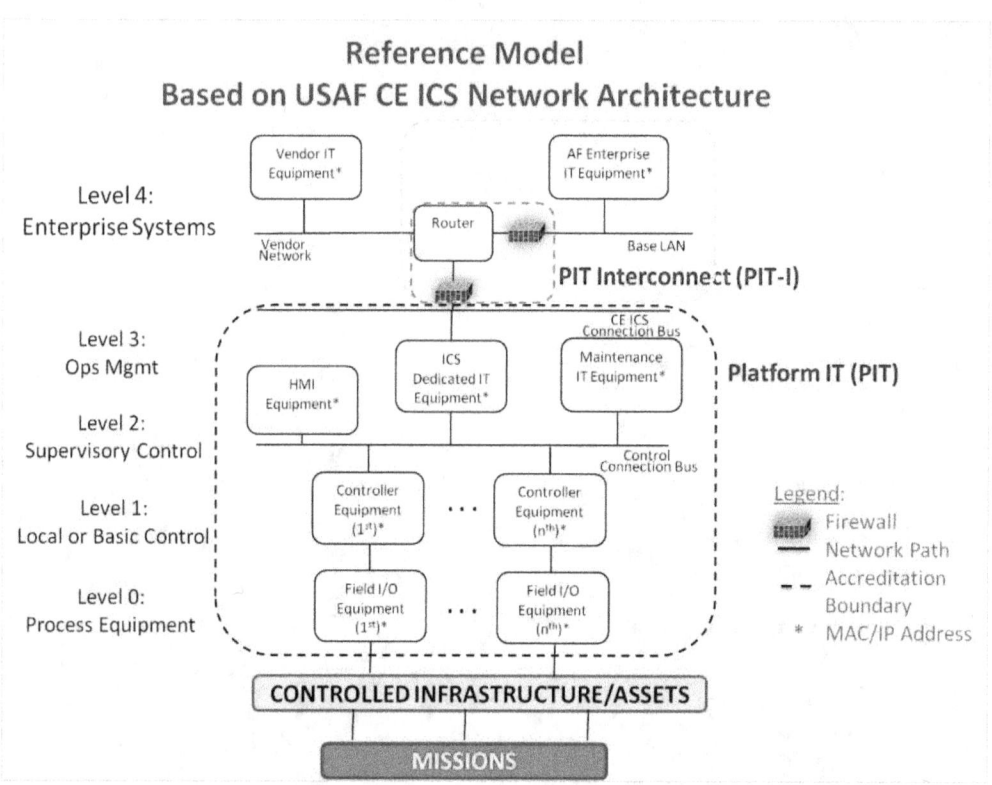

Extracted from selected publications as representative of varying approaches for modeling the basic process of risk management. Numerous varieties exist. Figures F1–F4 illustrate these varieties.

F1. DCIP Risk Management Process Model copied from DODI 3020.45, (p. 16).

Figure E3.F1. DCIP Risk Management Process Model*

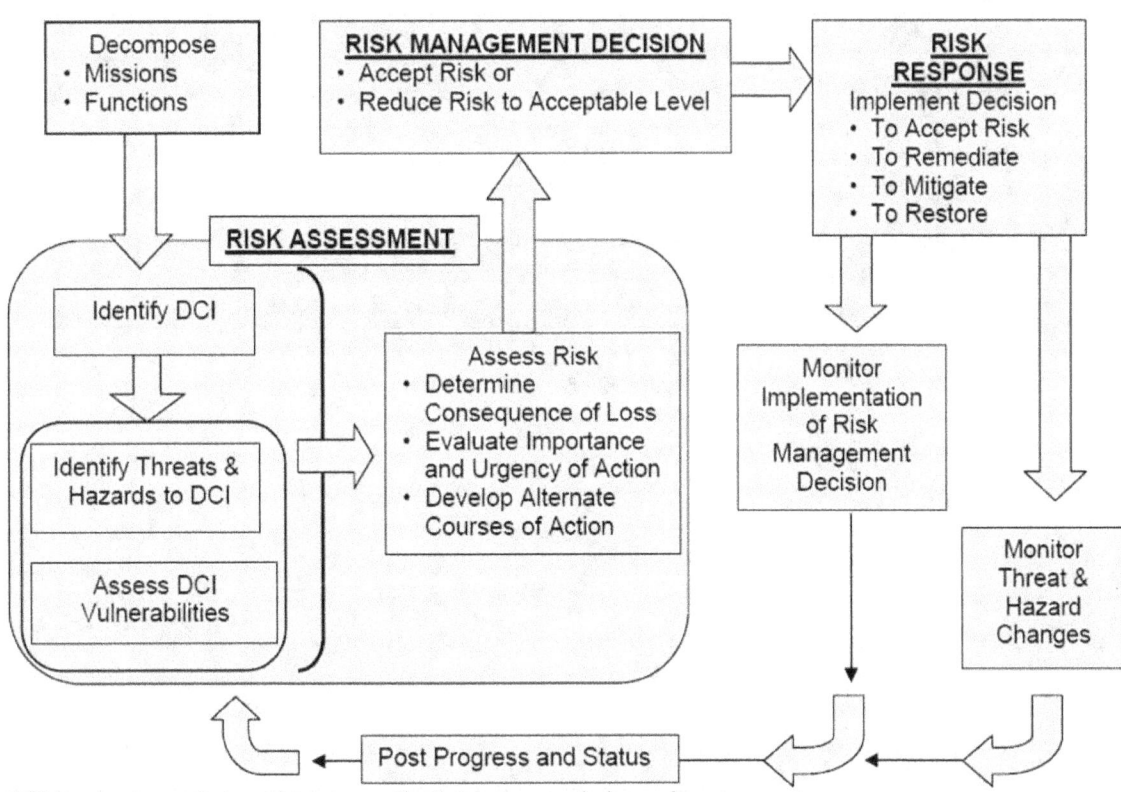

* This process requires continuous coordination between mission and asset owners

Figure F1. DODI 3020.45

F2. Risk Assessment Model as represented in NIST SP 800-30 (Rev. 1, Draft, 2011), (p. 7).

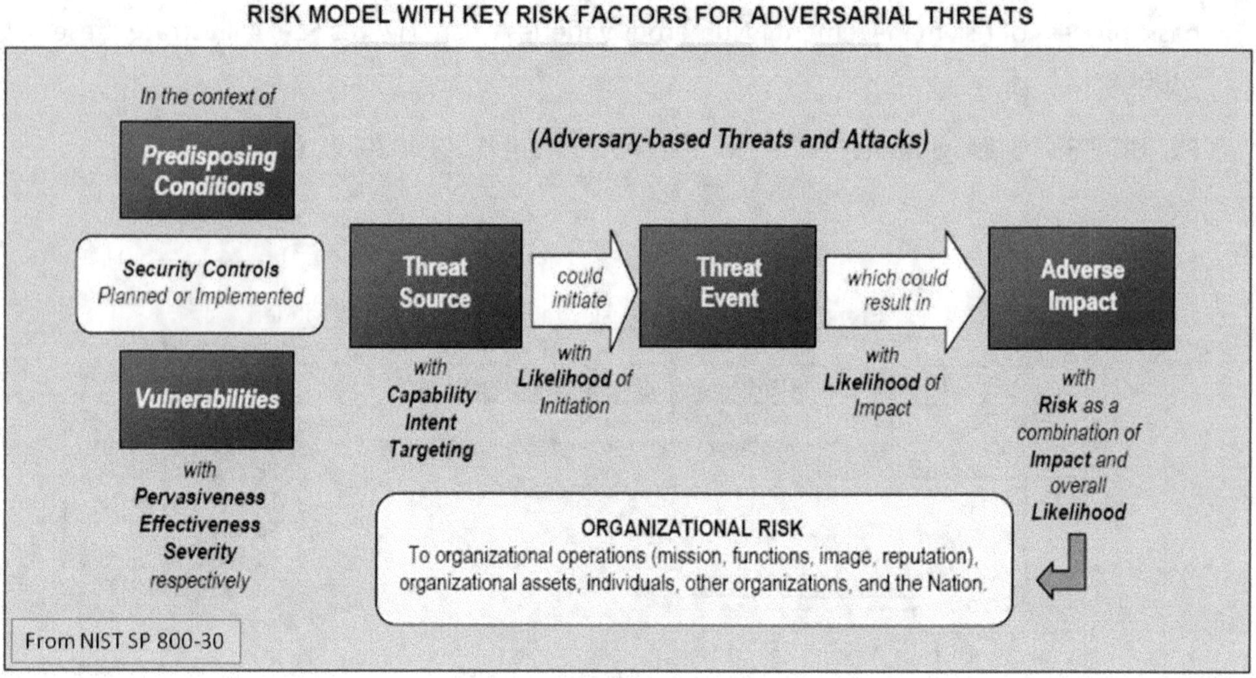

Figure F2. NIST SP 800-30

F3. Risk Management Process model depicted in ISO 31000, (p. 14).

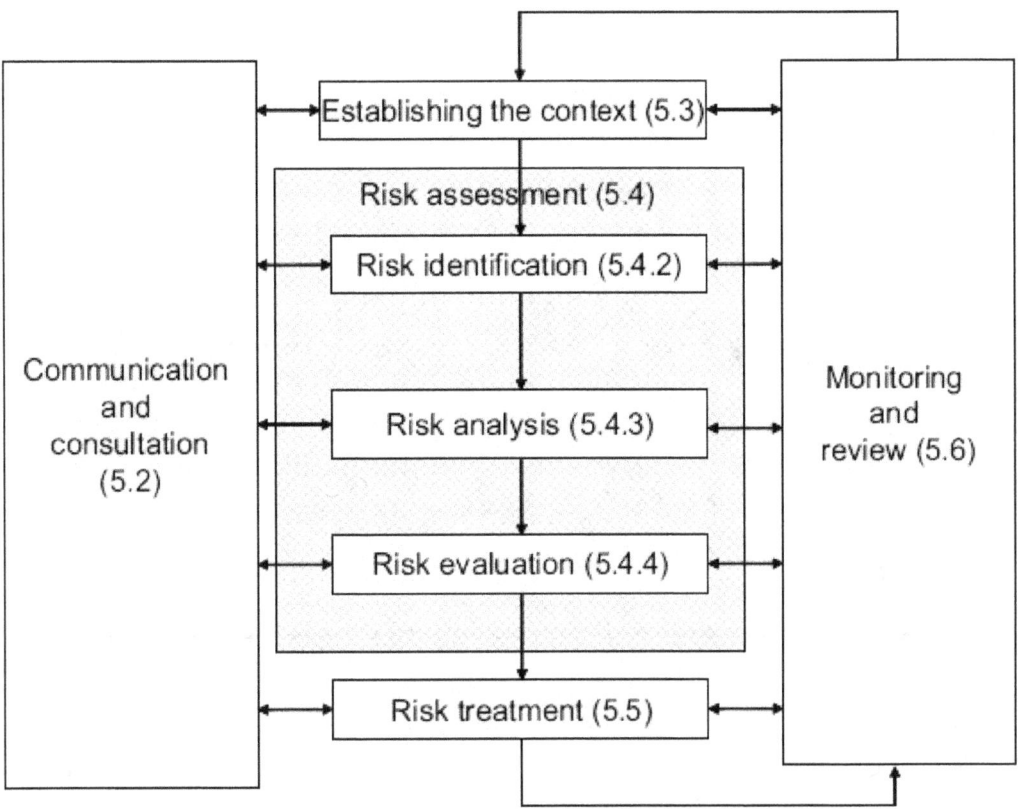

Figure F3. ISO 31000

F4. Generic model of risk assessment process.

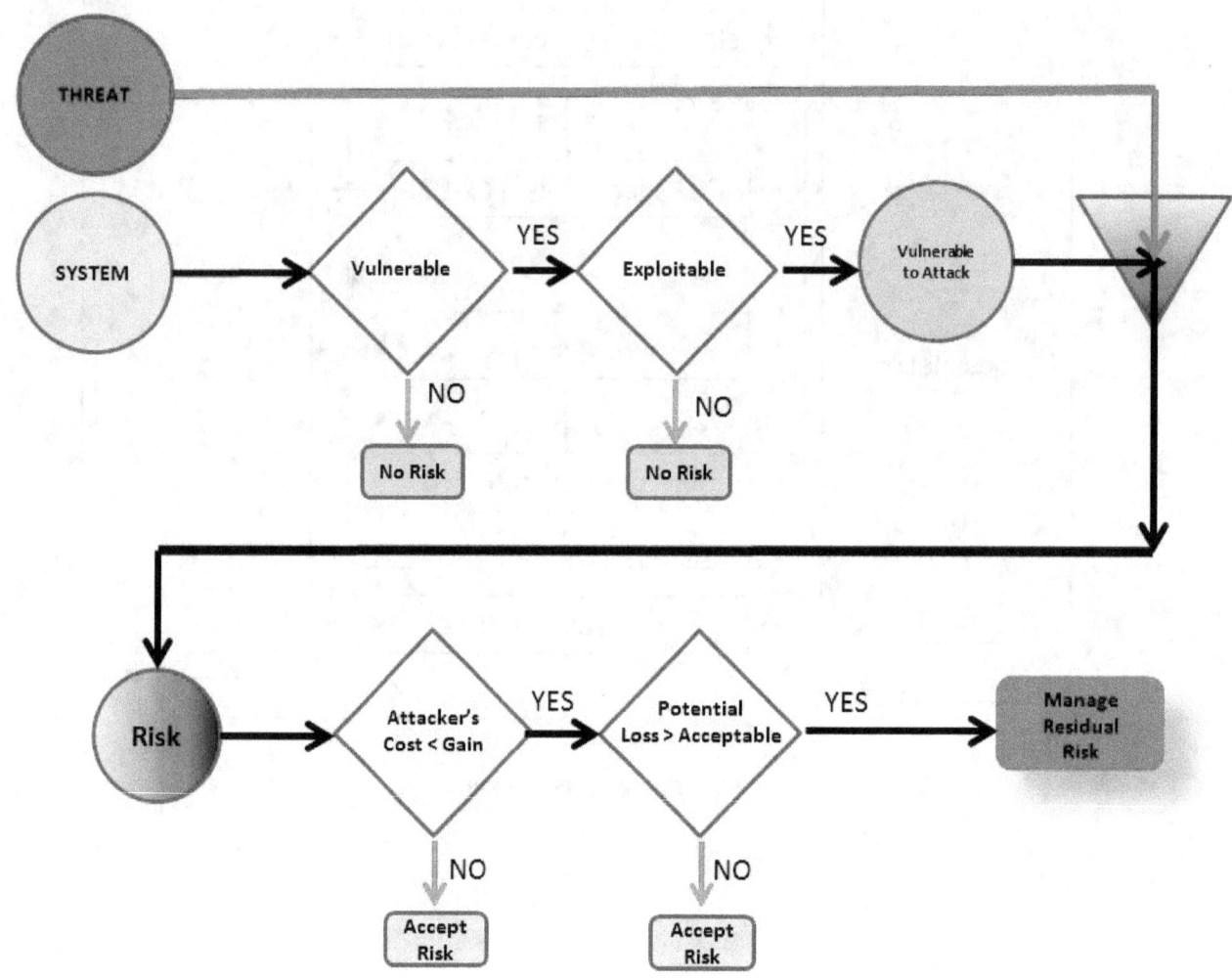

Figure F4. Generic Risk Assessment Process

CYBER SECURITY EVALUATION TOOL (CSET)

[Following extracted from the ICS-CERT web site. http://www.us-cert.gov/control_systems/satool.html *]*

The Cyber Security Evaluation Tool (CSET™) is a Department of Homeland Security (DHS) product that assists organizations in protecting their key national cyber assets. It was developed under the direction of the DHS National Cyber Security Division (NCSD) by cybersecurity experts and with assistance from the National Institute of Standards and Technology. This tool provides users with a systematic and repeatable approach for assessing the security posture of their cyber systems and networks. It includes both high-level and detailed questions related to all industrial control and IT systems. CSET is a desktop software tool that guides users through a step-by-step process to assess their control system and information technology network security practices against recognized industry standards. The output from CSET is a prioritized list of recommendations for improving the cybersecurity posture of the organization's enterprise and industrial control cyber systems. The tool derives the recommendations from a database of cybersecurity standards, guidelines, and practices. Each recommendation is linked to a set of actions that can be applied to enhance cybersecurity controls.

A caveat provided by the ICS-CERT: CSET is only one component of the overall cyber security picture and should be complemented with a robust cyber security program within the organization. A self-assessment with CSET cannot reveal all types of security weaknesses, and should not be the sole means of determining an organization's security posture. The tool will not provide an architectural analysis of the network or a detailed network hardware/software configuration review. It is not a risk analysis tool so it will not generate a complex risk assessment. CSET is not intended as a substitute for in depth analysis of control system vulnerabilities as performed by trained professionals.

SAMPLE QUESTION FROM CSET

Question 12.   Is a disaster recovery plan prepared, tested, and available in the event of a major hardware or software failure or destruction of the facility? Check all that apply.

Result	Answer(s)
	Not answered
Fail	None of the controls are implemented.

Pass	A disaster recovery plan (DRP) is available and is tested.
	Critical replacements for hard-to-obtain components are kept in inventory.
	The DRP includes a communication procedure and list of personnel to contact in the case of an emergency including ICS vendors, network administrators, ICS support personnel, etc.
	The DRP includes a complete and up-to-date logical network diagram.
	The DRP includes an authorized personnel list of those required for the ICS operations and maintenance.
	The DRP includes current configuration information for all components.
	The DRP includes procedures for operating the ICS in manual mode until secure conditions are restored.
	The DRP includes process and procedures for backup and secure storage of information.
	The DRP includes required response to events that activate the recovery plan.
	The DRP includes roles and responsibilities of responders.
	The DRP indicates requirements for the timely replacement of components in the case of an emergency.

Level Specific Requirement: [*part of the sample question*]

A disaster recovery plan is essential to continued availability of the ICS. The DRP should include the following items: Required response to events or conditions of varying duration and severity that would activate the recovery plan; Procedures for operating the ICS in manual mode with all external electronic connections severed until secure conditions can be restored; Roles and responsibilities of responders; Processes and procedures for the backup and secure storage of information; Complete and up-to-date logical network diagram; Personnel list for authorized physical and cyber access to the ICS; Communication procedure and list of personnel to contact in the case of an emergency including ICS vendors, network administrators, ICS support personnel, etc.; Current configuration information for all components.

The plan should also indicate requirements for the timely replacement of components in the case of an emergency. If possible, replacements for hard-to-obtain critical components should be kept in inventory.

DEFENSE CRITICAL INFRASTRUCTURE PROGRAM (DCIP)

[*verbatim extract from the DCIP web site* http://dcip.dtic.mil/index.html]

DCIP is an integrated risk management program designed to support DOD Mission Assurance programs. When effectively applied, these programs form a comprehensive structure to secure critical assets, infrastructure, and key resources for our nation. The nation's defense and economic vitality is highly dependent upon the availability and reliability of both DOD and non-DOD owned critical infrastructure (such as: power, transportation, telecommunications, water supply, etc.). With limited resources to address risk to critical infrastructure, the DCIP relies on continuous analysis of changing vulnerabilities to all types of threats and hazards to effectively manage risk to the nation's most essential infrastructure.

Recognizing how critical the infrastructure is to accomplishing DOD's missions and the effects of vulnerabilities to threats and hazards of infrastructure assets, DOD Directive 3020.40, *DOD Policy and Responsibility for Critical Infrastructure,* established the Defense Critical Infrastructure Program (DCIP), a program responsible for coordinating the management of risk to the critical infrastructure that DOD relies upon to execute its missions.

Increased global connectivity and interdependencies create numerous and changing vulnerabilities. Threats to "soft" targets do not only occur through criminal or terrorist activities, but also through national disasters, accidents, hazardous weather, and other natural and man-made events. Our national military strength and economic vitality is highly dependent upon the availability and reliability of both DOD and non-DOD owned critical infrastructure (such as: power, transportation, telecommunications, water supply, etc.) However, resources to address these vulnerabilities are limited and must be channeled to those deemed the highest priority. Additionally, priorities change as threats, vulnerabilities, and mission requirements evolve.

Relevant publications include:
DODD 3020.40, *DOD Policy and Responsibilities for Critical Infrastructure*
DODI 3020.45, *Defense Critical Infrastructure Program (DCIP) Management*
DODM 3020.45 Vol 1, *DCIP: DOD Mission-Based Critical Asset Identification Process (CAIP)*
DODI 5240.19, *Counterintelligence Support to the DCIP*
CJCSI 3209.01, *Defense Critical Infrastructure Program*
SECNAVINST 3501.1B, *Department of the Navy Critical Infrastructure Protection Program*
MCO 3501.36A, *Marine Corps Critical Infrastructure Program (MCCIP)*
AR 525-26, [Army] *Infrastructure Risk Management*
AFPD 10-24, *Air Force Critical Infrastructure Program (CIP)*

UJTs Relevant to Securing Critical Infrastructure

Universal Joint Tasks (UJT) provide the foundation upon which METs are constructed. The following selected UJTs are verbatim from the UJT List (UJTL) database found on the Joint Doctrine, Education & Training Electronic Information System (JDEIS).[36] The selection is not meant to be all-inclusive but representative and is provided merely to highlight the link between installation-level activities to secure ICS and national-level requirements.

SN 3.3.6.1 Assess Critical Infrastructure (CI) Impacts to Operational Capability

Determine the operational impacts resulting from the loss, disruption, and/or degradation of mission critical infrastructure.

Note: This task includes identifying the critical infrastructure and assets that are components of systems supporting all assigned missions; analyzing the potential consequences of a global event; assessing potential impacts to critical infrastructure and assets supporting assigned missions; and reporting results of the analysis and assessment.

SN 6.6.7.2 Conduct Defense Critical Infrastructure Program Analysis

To perform program management responsibilities including identification of defense critical infrastructures, perform risk analysis of vulnerabilities and mitigation, develop and maintain a predictive analysis capability to forecast and mitigate failure of critical assets early on. Seek input from the Defense Critical Infrastructure Program (CIP) sectors and report suspicious activities at specific facilities to appropriate Department of Defense and other governmental authorities.

ST 6.6.3 Manage Mission Risk Resulting From Defense Critical Infrastructure (DCI) Vulnerabilities

To manage actions taken at combatant command level to reduce the risk of mission degradation or failure, induced by known vulnerabilities of defense critical assets, infrastructure, or functional capability.

ST 6.6.4 Prevent or Mitigate the Loss or Degradation of Critical Assets

To allocate resources to reduce or offset asset vulnerabilities from all hazards, man-made, and natural threats.

---

[36] https://jdeis.js.mil/jdeis/index.jsp?pindex=43

ST 6.6 Perform Mission Assurance

Maintain plans and programs to ensure assigned tasks or duties can be performed IAW the intended purpose or plan.

Note: This task focuses on fully integrating a mission-focused process to understand and protect physical and information capabilities critical to performance of assigned missions at the strategic theater level of war. It links risk management program activities and security related functions -- such as force protection; antiterrorism; critical infrastructure protection; information assurance; continuity of operations; chemical, biological, radiological, nuclear and high-explosive defense; readiness and installation preparedness -- to create the synergistic effect required for the Department of Defense to mobilize, deploy, support, and sustain military operations throughout the continuum of operations.

OP 6.7 Conduct Defense Critical Infrastructure Protection Program

To conduct coordination between individuals charged with day-to-day operation and maintenance of DCI/As and the individuals charged with infrastructure investment strategies.

OP 6.7.1 Identify Task Critical Assets

To identify mission-critical assets and associate them with a particular facility.

OP 6.7.2 Coordinate Task Critical Asset Vulnerability Assessment

To conduct a systematic examination of mission-essential systems, assets, and applications, to identify vulnerabilities, which could cause a degradation or loss (incapacity to perform designed function) as a result of being subjected to a certain level of threat or hazard.

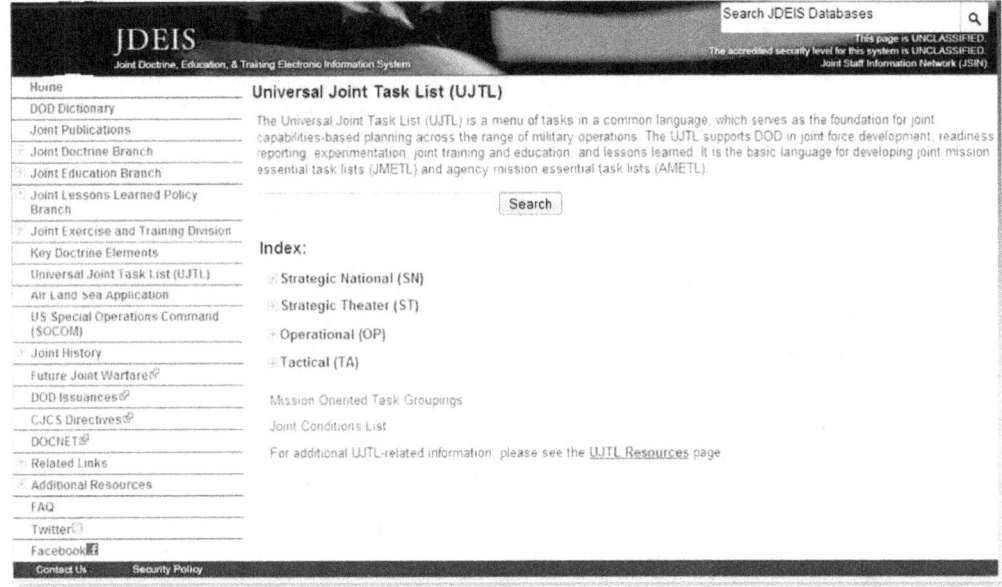

Training on various aspects of ICS to include security is available from numerous providers and in a variety of venues. The following samples are by no means all-inclusive but represent the variety of vendors and venues. Descriptions are from the vendors' or sponsors' web sites. For those not overly familiar with ICS, an excellent starting point is the US-CERT's web-based "Cyber Security for Control Systems Engineers & Operators" (link below). In spite of the course title, it is not necessary to be either an engineer or an ICS operator to gain valuable fundamental understanding about ICS security in a very short time.

US-CERT (http://www.us-cert.gov/control_systems/cstraining.html)
- **Web-based Training**
  The following summary level courses are available for on-line training:
  OPSEC for Control Systems
  Cyber Security for Control Systems Engineers & Operators
- **Instructor Led format - Introductory Level**
  Introduction to Control Systems Cybersecurity (101) - 1 day or 8 hrs
  ICS Security for Management (111) - 1 - 2 hrs
- **Instructor Led format - Intermediate Level**
  Intermediate Cybersecurity for Industrial Control Systems (201) - lecture only - 1 day or 8 hrs
- **Hands-on format - Intermediate Technical Level**
  Intermediate Cybersecurity for Industrial Control Systems (202) - with lab/exercises - 1 day or 8 hrs
- **Hands-on format - Advanced Technical Level**
  ICS Advanced Cybersecurity (301) - 5 days
- The Control Systems Security Program (CSSP) provides training courses and workshops at various industry association events. These courses are packed with up-to-date information on cyber threats and mitigations for vulnerabilities. I f your organization would like to learn more about training opportunities, please contact cssp_training@hq.dhs.gov.

Sandia National Laboratories (http://energy.sandia.gov/?page_id=6912)
SCADA Assessment Training Course: Methodologies for assessing SCADA systems and an overview of related security and vulnerability concerns
This customizable course covers a breadth of SCADA and other digital control system use in infrastructures and industry, identifies vulnerabilities of these components and systems, and presents methodologies and tools to assess these systems in a successful, measurable, reproducible manner. It is being offered to other groups on a limited basis in order to improve the security of infrastructures and systems critical to the United States. This

course is offered at Sandia's discretion to individuals with need-to-know and by invitation only.

Idaho National Laboratory (http://www.inl.gov/scada/training/)

The following courses are available through Idaho National Laboratory NSTB program. All the courses are designed to increase cyber security awareness and defensive capabilities for IT/Control System managers, IT/Control System security personnel, network and control system support engineers, and control system designers and developers who are involved in or responsible for control system cyber security. The courses are geared toward systems in the energy sector, but are relevant to most control system environments. The 4- and 8-hour courses are certified for NERC continuing education credits.

- Introductory SCADA Security (4 hours)
- Intermediate SCADA Security (8 hours)
- Advanced SCADA Security Red/Blue Team (5 days)

Air Force Institute of Technology
(http://www.afit.edu/CESS/Course_Desc.cfm?p=WTSS%20580)

COURSE: **WTSS 580 Managing Security of Control Systems**

OBJECTIVE: To assess vulnerabilities for control systems' environment for people, processes, and technology and recommend improved security strategies.

DESCRIPTION: This course explores a wide range of people, processes, and technology issues in the management of critical infrastructure control systems (CS) security including Supervisory Control and Data Acquisition (SCADA) systems security. Systems monitoring and controlling base-level and regional supply and flow of resources such as electricity, water, gas, and transportation are examined. Topics include CS components, threats, and vulnerability assessment and technical measures for improving security peculiar CS, such as multifactor authentication, telephony firewalls and radio frequency encryption, and operational and physical security. The CS industry and initiatives in CS security standards are explored. This includes focus on the interplay between regional commercial providers and base-level continuity of operations. The move toward integration of CS with traditional computer networks is covered.

INFOSEC Institute (http://www.infosecinstitute.com/courses/scada_security_online.html)

SCADA Security Online: SCADA, DCS, and other process control networks, generically called SCADA, run the nation's mission critical infrastructure, everything from the power grid to water treatment, chemical manufacturing to transportation. These networks are at increasing risk due to the move to standard protocols, the Microsoft OS and interconnection to other networks. Learn the skills required to direct and manage the appropriate cyber security protection for your SCADA system.

SANS Institute (http://www.sans.org)
- **Intermediate SCADA Security: Department of Energy**: National SCADA Test Bed Program (Hands-on) - This fast-paced course covers general control system cyber security challenges. The training objectives include looking at the risk equation (threat, vulnerability and consequences) and how they relate to the control system environment. Who are the threat actors? What vulnerabilities exist in the control system space? What can be the consequences of exploitation? What mitigation strategies can be implemented to help protect the control system environment?
- **SCADA Security Advanced Training**: This five-day course combines advanced topics from SCADA and IT security into the first hands-on Ethical Hacking course for ICS. Both SCADA Administrators and IT Security Professionals will widen their knowledge through hands-on exercises with live SCADA systems and equipment.

Sampling of other vendors (*caveat emptor*):
- Lofty Perch (https://www.loftyperch.com/index/use_lang/EN/page/401.html)
- SCADAhacker (http://scadahacker.com/training.html)
- Red Tiger (http://www.redtigersecurity.com/)
- TONEX (http://www.tonex.com/Courses/194/1499/)
- Digital Bond (https://www.digitalbond.com)--but not accessible from .mil domain

US-CERT
UNITED STATES COMPUTER EMERGENCY READINESS TEAM

HOME   SECURITY PUBLICATIONS   ALERTS AND TIPS   RELATED RESOURCES   ABOUT US   GFIRST

Control Systems

Home
Calendar
ICS-CERT
ICSJWG
Information Products
Training
Recommended Practices
Secure Architecture Design
Assessments
Standards & References
Related Sites
FAQ

Control Systems Security Program (CSSP)

Training available through CSSP

Scheduled training is on the CSSP Calendar.

Web-based Training
The following summary level courses are available for on-line training
OPSEC for Control Systems
Cyber Security for Control Systems Engineers & Operators

Instructor Led format - Introductory Level
Introduction to Control Systems Cybersecurity (101) - 1 day or 8 hrs
ICS Security for Management (111) - 1 - 2 hrs

Instructor Led format - Intermediate Level
Intermediate Cybersecurity for Industrial Control Systems (201) - lecture only - 1 day or 8 hrs

Hands-on format - Intermediate Technical Level
Intermediate Cybersecurity for Industrial Control Systems (202) - with lab/exercises - 1 day or 8 hrs

Hands-on format - Advanced Technical Level
ICS Advanced Cybersecurity (301) - 5 days

The Control Systems Security Program provides training courses and workshops at various industry association events
These courses are packed with up-to-date information on cyber threats and mitigations for vulnerabilities. If your
organization would like to learn more about training opportunities, please contact cssp_training@hq.dhs.gov

Organizations Engaged on ICS Security

The following organizations can advise and assist with ICS vulnerability and risk assessments mostly using their own sets of tools and SMEs. This is merely a subset of a broader community engaged on ICS security.

ICS-CERT   http://www.us-cert.gov/control_systems/ics-cert/
The Industrial Control Systems Cyber Emergency Response Team (ICS-CERT) [Dept of Homeland Defense] provides a control system security focus in collaboration with US-CERT to:
- respond to and analyze control systems related incidents,
- conduct vulnerability and malware analysis,
- provide on-site support for incident response and forensic analysis,
- provide situational awareness in the form of actionable intelligence,
- coordinate the responsible disclosure of vulnerabilities/mitigations, and
- share and coordinate vulnerability information and threat analysis through information products and alerts.

AFCESA   http://www.afcesa.af.mil/
The Air Force Civil Engineering Support Agency (HQ USAF/A7C) [USAF-centric], CEO Division, provides (on a scheduled basis) specialized ICS and IT teams to apply the ICS PIT C&A Program. AFCESA/CEO's standard procedure is to apply the risk assessment program at Air Force-managed installations on a scheduled basis, with a goal of revisitation every three years; they may visit out-of-cycle on an as-requested basis but will be constrained by already-scheduled assessments. As of this publication, the AFCESA C&A teams operate under authority of SAF/CIO A6, and in accordance with DODI 8500.01E, AFI 33-210, and AFCESA ETL 11-1.

262 NWS   http://washingtonairguard.org/194rsw/
The 262d Network Warfare Squadron (262 NWS) is an Air National Guard (ANG) unit operating on Joint Base Lewis-McChord, near Tacoma, Washington. The Washington ANG web site reflects: Nationally recognized as a Cyber Warfare leader, the 262 NWS conducts worldwide network security operations to improve the DOD GiG and the Air Force's network security posture. Recent high-level assessments include the White House Communications Agency, US Central Command, Space Command, and European Command. They also participate in on-going responses to Air Force and DOD cyber incidents, all amidst an increasing number of federal- and state-directed assessments.

NSTB   http://www.inl.gov/scada/

To ensure the secure, reliable and efficient distribution of power, the DOE jointly established the National SCADA Test Bed (NSTB) program at INL and SNL. The program works to support industry and government efforts to enhance the cyber security of control systems used throughout the electricity, oil, and gas industries. Among the services available: Control system security product and technology assessments to identify vulnerabilities and corresponding mitigation approaches.

IDART   http://idart.sandia.gov/

The Information Design Assurance Red Team (IDART) provides independent, objective, adversary-based assessments of information, communication, and critical infrastructure systems throughout their lifecycle (concept through retirement) in order to identify vulnerabilities and threats, improve design, and assist decision makers with choices in the development, security, and use of their systems. [*Operates out of Sandia National Laboratory.*]

> "The greatest strength of a 21st century grid—evolving technology—may also present opportunities for additional vulnerabilities. Networks of computers, intelligent electronic devices, software, and communication technologies present greater infrastructure protection challenges than those of the traditional infrastructure. Notably, a smarter grid includes more devices and connections that may become avenues for intrusions, error-caused disruptions, malicious attacks, destruction, and other threats."
>
> *A Policy Framework for the 21st Century Grid (p. 49)*

With reference to the eight-step process introduced at the beginning of this handbook, this section will facilitate the following activities:

- **Mission analysis**
- **ID assets**
- **Determine ICS dependencies**
- **Determine ICS connectivity**
- **Assess risk**
- **Prioritize risk management actions**

This leaves the following activities to be addressed by the installation ICS security team.

- **Implement actions**
- **Monitor and reenter the cycle as required**

<u>Roles and Responsibilities</u>

Facilitator

The Installation Commander should appoint a facilitator for this data collection. The results from this effort will assist in determining priorities for resource commitment decisions. The facilitator will have the following responsibilities:

- Authority to gather the required data
- Assembling the experts related to infrastructures that support the missions
- Collating data related to the system dependencies
- Documenting the dependencies of systems, infrastructures, and interconnections (spreadsheet, database, diagrams, etc.)

The duration of this effort depends on the depth of knowledge and documentation of the existing systems. Documenting processes that do not exist, have been abandoned, or were never installed will diminish the value of this. Rigor should be applied to the process of ensuring the dependencies and interconnects are characterized as precisely as possible. This activity also may need to be iterative; a lightning strike knocking out power may expose a connection that was unknown, at which point the diagram/table should be updated as this will alter the relative importance values. The initial amount of time to allocate would be one hour per infrastructure or one-half day for a large meeting with several infrastructures. The facilitated meetings (combined) should not take more than one day for each mission. Additional time can be determined based on the outcome of the first session. Incomplete groups of data can be collected and documented. Gaps should be noted and filled as experts or data become available.

CAVEAT: Some data may require a clearance to obtain and may result in generating classified documents. A derivative classifier or classification authority should be consulted prior to beginning this effort. The documentation will be, at a minimum, "For Official Use Only."

Some data may not be obtainable. Remember, this is not documenting <u>how</u> the processes work; this is documenting the <u>mission dependencies on processes and systems</u> that in turn depend on one another. Here are examples of utilities and infrastructures that should be part of this effort:

- Electricity
- Fuel
- Water/Waste Water
- Natural Gas
- Security (gates, doors, surveillance, etc.)
  - If security is the mission, then ensure security and the systems/networks security uses are represented in the diagram. If security is a mitigating measure, then make notation of this. Essentially, if the doors lock due to a power outage of the security system, can the mission still function?
- Lights (emergency, runway, search, etc.)
- Emergency Services
- Communications (networks, wired, wireless)
- People (groups, organizations, contractors, etc.)
- Control systems, SCADA systems, HVAC systems, etc.

Subject Matter Experts

The utilities and infrastructures listed above involve people who have expert knowledge about how they connect to other systems or what systems they depend on. They will be supplying the data that builds the diagram/table discussed below. How the system works will sometimes supply additional information on the dependencies and interdependencies.

Example: If the entire water system depends on one electrical feed, then the details of how the water system works will not be as useful as the fact that there is one electrical connection. If the details of the water system identify which HVAC, waste water, potable water, and electrical generation systems depend on the water, then those details are indicating downstream dependencies that need to be documented.

To focus all participants on the objective of this activity, the facilitator may have to make leading statements or ask pointed questions such as:

- "If power were cut, how long can you remain operational?"
- "If the temperature in this building reaches 90 degrees, will the equipment remain functional?"
- "If a <insert disaster> destroyed the <insert part of the building>, would that impact our <insert infrastructure>?"

Using the Diagram

The following figure (Figure Atch1-1) is a representation of a fictitious mission. Each hexagon represents a system or process boundary. The connections between the systems indicate dependencies. The numeric values represent the relative value to one another starting with a base value of 1 for the mission and escalating with each dependency. The rules for escalating the value will be discussed later in this section. Looking at this figure, what system or group of systems has the highest value? Are they inside or outside of the jurisdiction boundary?

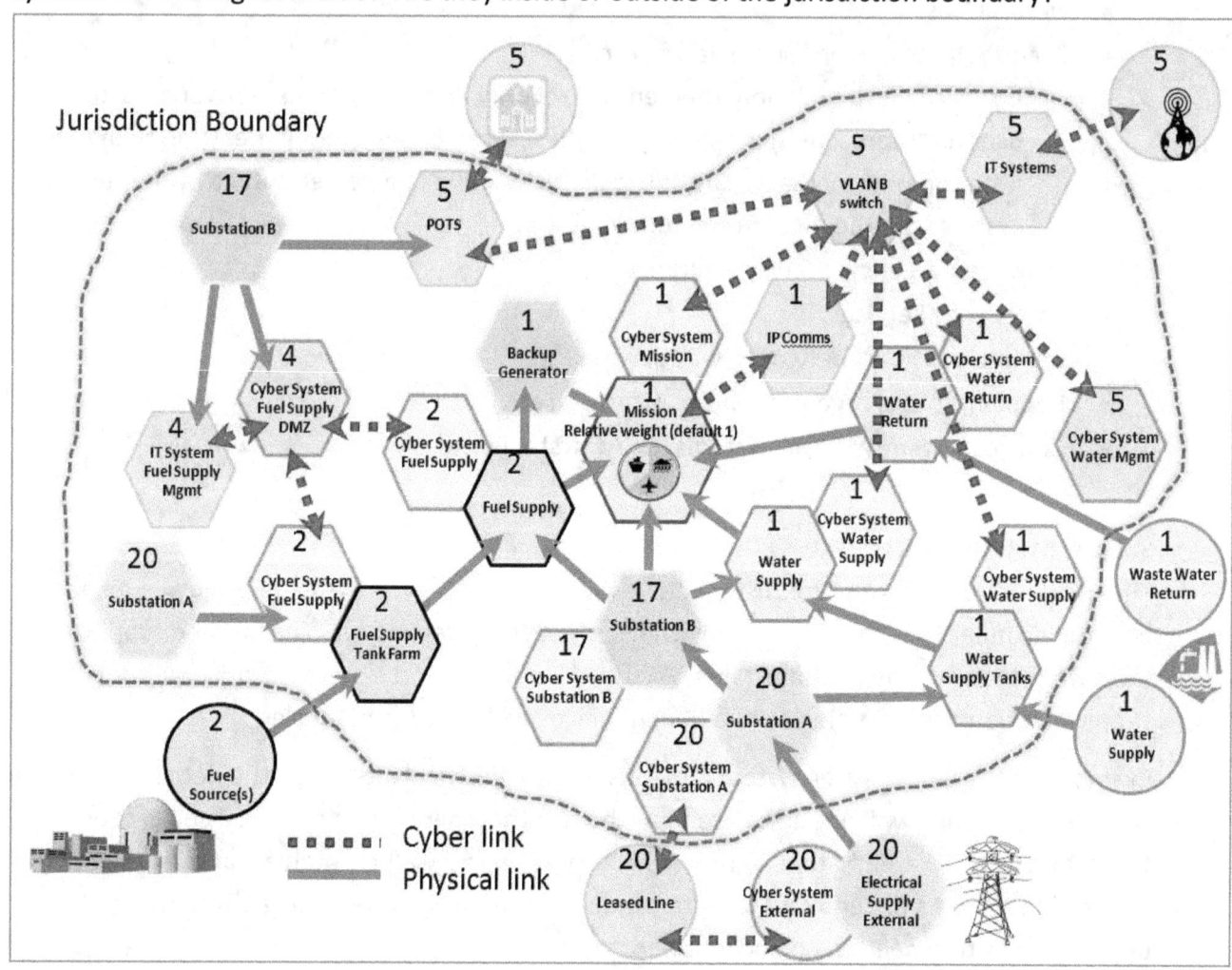

Figure Atch1-1. Example Mission Interdependencies

The figure has color coded hexagons to make finding items easier. For example, electrical systems are blue with a yellow outline. The cyber systems (control systems) associated with the electrical systems are indicated as their own green hexagons. The electrical systems located at the center bottom of the figure have the highest relative importance. The leased line, electrical supply, substation A, and their associated cyber systems (control systems) all have values of 20. The quick meaning is that without electricity, the rest of the systems are likely to be non-functional. The pumps will no longer work to deliver fuel or water to the mission. The IT equipment will no longer be powered. The only item that would remain functional would be the backup generator located to the upper left of the mission (in the middle). This would allow the mission to function at least until the fuel for the backup generator was consumed.

Taking another look at the figure, in the upper-right corner there is a virtual local area network (VLAN) switch with quite a few connections. If there was found a vulnerability that allowed switching from one VLAN to another, could an intruder from the water cyber system get into the process cyber system? That VLAN switch concentrates a significant portion of the cyber traffic around that mission. As such, that component is fairly significant to the successful operation of the mission. The numeric value of 5 indicates the relative importance.

Without prior knowledge of the mission or how the systems operate, a determination can be made of the relative importance of the systems with a quick glance. Another potential representation of this data would be as a topological map imposed on the facility. The highest point would still be the electrical systems. When attempting to control or secure an area that is on low ground surrounded by high ground, are defenses placed on the low ground or the high ground? This diagram and method for generating this diagram should help make that decision, back that decision up with numeric values based on the infrastructure in place, and then apply resources as the installation commander sees fit.

Rules for the Mapping of Interdependencies

The following definitions will be useful:

- *Missions* are comprised of *functions*
- *Functions* have requirements in terms of *utilities*, *systems*, and *people*
- *Utilities*, *systems*, and *people* have requirements as they are supplied by additional layers
- *Systems/Process* – An object/component or group of objects/components that accomplish a result
- *Object / Component* – An item or group of items that accomplish a task
  - A valve, PLC, temperature indicator, and computer are all components. A system would be the combination of all of them together performing HVAC. A pumping station may comprise of several pumps, controllers, communications, and power components.
  - Sometimes an object or component is a system in and of itself. A managed switch may be necessary to break out as a system boundary because it intersects several networks and segments them with VLANs.

Each layer beyond the initial layer of utilities, systems, and people may comprise a system in and of itself that needs to be identified by the boundaries. Two separated control systems running two segmented parts of a system would be two different representations linked by a process system physical connection. Physical and cyber systems should not be combined so the impacts to one can be seen on the other. The cyber system should be attached and will inherit the value from the process. An example is shown in Figure Atch1-2 below. The SCADA/ICS cyber systems may have several network boundaries they traverse, this is also shown in the figure where the system on Substation A and the system on Electrical Supply External are using a Leased Line to communicate. The Leased Line is owned by a different group and the communications between the two systems depends on it. It is not uncommon to have shared data highways, such as a fiber optic ring, that infrastructure use to communicate. Treat shared interconnects (e.g., a fiber optic ring with the associated switch gear) as a system/process.

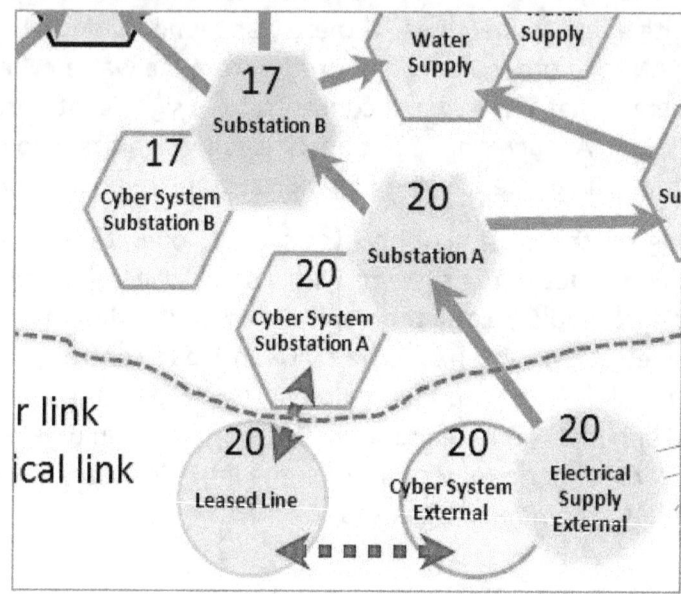

Figure Atch1-2. ICS Representation

Use the following types of diagrams and drawings to assist in creating the interdependency diagram:

- Network diagrams
- Cabinet drawings
- Electrical drawings
- Process diagrams
- Site location diagrams

Use names or locations for tie-in points to components that are connected to multiple components or the diagram may become overly cumbersome. An example of what to do is shown in Figure Atch1-3. The VLANB switch has multiple cyber connections that overlap other systems. While this does represent the connections, this can make the diagram difficult to read.

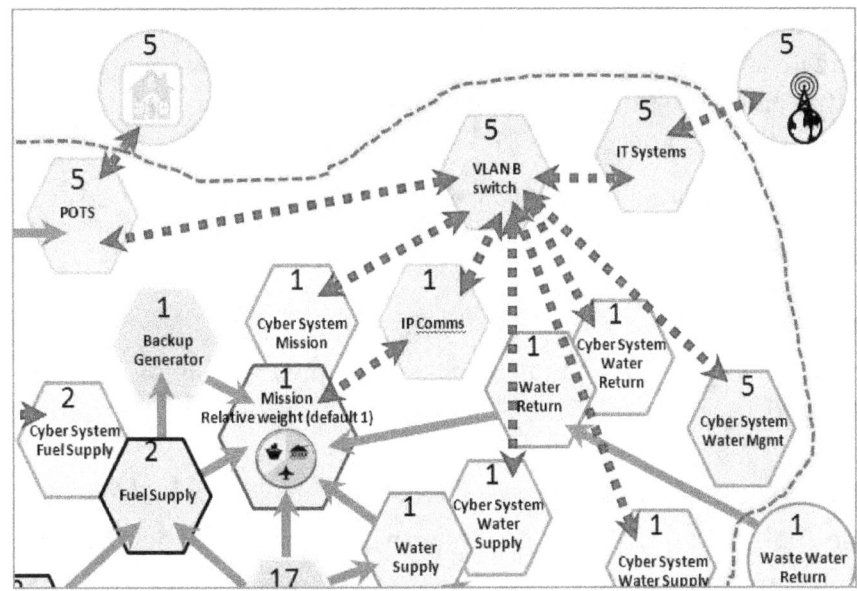

Figure Atch1-3. Congested Dependencies

An alternative way of representing multiple connections is to make an additional object with the same name and make the dependency connections. The difficulty in this solution is in finding the partners. In Figure Atch1-4, both Substation A and Substation B are split in order to keep the diagram cleaner. Network boundaries are also shown in Figure Atch1-4. The cyber systems for the Fuel Supply have a DMZ network with which they both communicate. The DMZ network then has an additional network that it communicates with where the data from the Fuel Supply systems is accessed. A historian passing data to an archive server on an IT network is an example of this type of architecture.

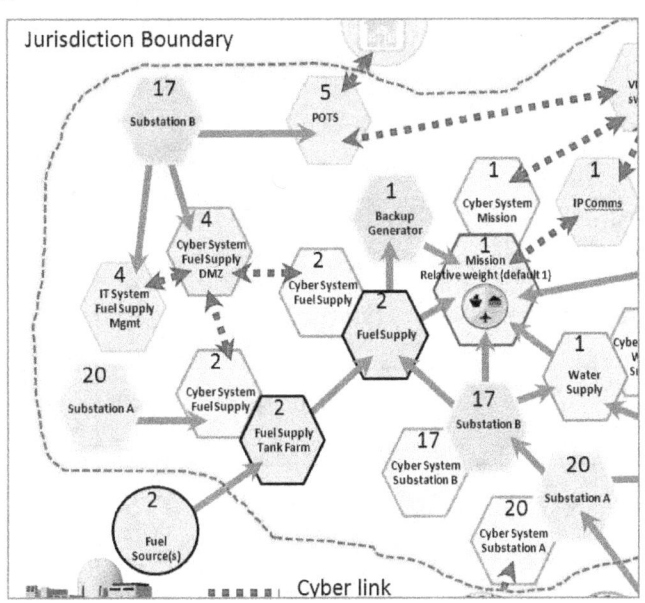

Figure Atch1-4. Decongested Dependencies

The diagram itself should show the dependencies of each system relative to the mission going outward until the installation commander reaches a point where he/she no longer has ownership. At that point, the system dependencies end as indicated by circles in the diagrams above.

The numeric values are assigned to each process or system based on this one rule.

- *A system inherits the values of all of those systems that depend on it.*
  - *The mission value is set to 1.*
  - *All other systems derive their values from the mission value.*
  - *Circular connections are handled consistently (choose to either add them or do not add them)*

The easiest way of generating these values is to use a database or a table in Excel. An example table is shown in Table Atch1-1. Do not generate these values while determining dependencies. Attempting to do so will not benefit the facilitated meeting. The table should contain these columns: *Process/System Boundary, Zi (relative importance), Dependants*, and *geographical information services (GIS) coordinates of the Process/System (optional).*

The cells should be linked as indicated by the cell references depicted. The geographical information services (GIS) data are the GIS coordinates of that component, they are optional. Zi is the aggregated impact or importance value of the component based on dependencies.

Table Atch1-1. **Example Relative Importance of Interdependent Systems**

	A	B	C	D	E	F	G	H
1	Process / System Boundary	GIS Data	Zi [=sum(D1...Dm)]	D1	D2	D3	D4	D5
2	Mission		1					
3	Cyber System Mission		=SUM(D3:H3)	=C2				
4	Backup Generator		=SUM(D4:H4)	=C2				
5	Fuel Supply		=SUM(D5:H5)	=C2	=C4			
6	Cyber System Fuel Supply		=SUM(D6:H6)	=C5				
7	Cyber System Fuel Supply DMZ		=SUM(D7:H7)	=C6	=C9			
8	IT System Fuel Supply Mgmt		=SUM(D8:H8)	=C7				
9	Cyber System Fuel Supply Tank Farm		=SUM(D9:H9)	=C10				

10	Fuel Supply Tank Farm		=SUM(D10:H10)	=C5				
11	Substation A		=SUM(D11:H11)	=C17	=C12	=C9		
12	Substation B		=SUM(D12:J12)	=C2	=C16	=C5	=C20	=C7
13	Cyber System Substation A		=SUM(D13:H13)	=C11				
14	Cyber System Substation B		=SUM(D14:H14)	=C12				
15	Leased Line		=SUM(D15:H15)	=C13				
16	Water Supply		=SUM(D16:H16)	=C2				
17	Water Supply Tanks		=SUM(D17:H17)	=C16				
18	Electrical Supply External		=SUM(D18:H18)	=C11				
19	Cyber System External Electrical Supply		=SUM(D19:H19)	=C18				

If this were mapped to a GIS map using an alternative elevation of the relative importance, the data would represent terrain that needs securing. The lower elevations are the items of interest and the areas of higher relative importance would be key locations to control the region. The scope of this project prevents the creation of a graphical tool kit so the variations of the graphical depiction will be based on the people contributing to this activity. A white board "exercise" would also work to create a physical image depicting the interdependencies.

Generating the diagram and table

The facilitator should use materials they have at hand. A large white board, poster-sized paper hung on the wall, or poster-sized paper on a tabletop are examples of suitable mediums.

1. Starting with the mission, draw an object and label it "mission" or use the proper mission name.
2. Describe the mission and its functions to the assembled experts and draw radial lines outward from the mission object to show dependencies.

Example: The facilitator makes the statement, "The mission is to provide bombers; which require maintenance, fuel, runways, ordinance, and crew." The facilitator draws radial lines outward connecting it to objects labeled "maintenance," "fuel,." "runways," "ordinance," and "crew."

3. The experts assembled should represent people knowledgeable about each function with which the mission relies. Some experts will know about several functions. In an

orderly fashion, capture everyone's input. Drawing objects and connecting lines to show the systems/processes and dependencies. Use arrows if the dependency is one way with the arrow pointing toward the downstream or consumer component. Resolve conflicts in a professional manner. Resolution may take the form of a field trip, a field test, or a discussion. If the resolution must be postponed until after the facilitated session, document the object with a question mark to show uncertainty.

NOTE: Computer networks should be viewed in a frame of consumer/publisher. What system produces the information and what system consumes the information. The consumer is dependent on the producer. The producer is not dependent on the consumer.

4. Document the diagram. This can be done by printing, photographing, or whatever means is suitable for the medium.
5. Generate a table of Relative Importance of Interdependent Systems based on the diagram.
6. The table will generate values for each system/process based on the documented dependencies.

Assessing the risk and prioritizing risk management actions

Assessing the risk and prioritizing the risk management actions on a macro scale requires a high-level determination of cyber risk. The purpose of the high-level determination is to prioritize areas of focus to perform more time consuming assessments. Performing this calculation will take into account how a system is used or monitored.

Calculation of Priority based on Use

Maintenance for mechanical devices is fairly well understood. There are differences in opinions on how best to perform maintenance. Cyber systems require a different kind of maintenance. The concern is the chance that, due to a lack of information technology maintenance, the control system will be an easier target for hacking. A quick search using the NIST National Vulnerability Database (http://nvd.nist.gov/view/vuln/search) is presented in Table Atch1-2. These are the rates of reporting, not necessarily the rate of discovery. Each product has the vulnerabilities it was created with; products do not create new vulnerabilities by existing. As interest in a system increases, the number of reported vulnerabilities increases. This is different from a mechanical device that wears out over time. Programs do not wear out, though the vendor may discontinue the product.

Table Atch1-2. Number of Reported Vulnerabilities

Company	Reported over 3 months	Reported over 3 years	Avg / Month
Oracle	185	984	27.3
Microsoft	83	876	24.3
Linux	121	855	23.8
Adobe	29	535	14.9
McAfee	1	25	0.7
Symantec	20	98	2.7
Invensys	7	14	0.4
ABB	6	47	1.3
Siemens	9	34	0.9
Cisco	56	473	13.1
Juniper	0	16	0.4
Dlink	1	10	0.3
Intel	11	138	3.8
AMD	2	9	0.3
NVIDIA	3	7	0.2
ATI	7	68	1.9
Dell	1	13	0.4

Access to a control system allows users to perform actions. Stuxnet showed how important this is. The vulnerabilities used by Stuxnet were not vulnerabilities in the Siemens software; they were vulnerabilities in the operating system. Once on the consoles, Stuxnet made use of the Siemens software to perform tasks it was designed to do. Any vulnerability that allows arbitrary execution of code can allow malicious software access to control system functions that are available to the user account the vulnerable program is using.

A control system uses three methods of user access control:

1. The first is no security. The software will run as the operating system account currently logged in. These types of systems often run as an administrative level user. If one can log into the console, one can perform any action on the system such as opening breakers or valves, adjusting set points, or downloading new configuration to the field controllers.

2. The second method is a custom user account manager on top of the operating system accounts. This method can result in security being turned on/off for the control system and circumstances where no user accounts exist for the control system thereby locking the console until it is rebuilt with an image or reinstalled. This method will typically use an auto-login account for the operating system and then have the operations personnel use their own custom user account to gain access to the control system interfaces. The auto-login account is often an administrative level user.

3. The third method is to use accounts integrated into the operating system user accounts. This is more common of systems designed after 2001. This will be a mix of user accounts with role-based privileges. A look at the processes running on the console will show a number of user accounts that are control-system specific that likely have administrative rights, which are used to keep key system functions operational.

This is why software management and system monitoring is important for control systems. Assume that the system can be compromised then watch the system for aberrant behavior indicating unstable code. Achieving this level of monitoring takes resources in the form of people, procedures, and technology. All of which cost money to deploy and maintain. In the previous section, the interdependencies of the infrastructure were determined and a table was built. The relative importance to the mission was determined for each system. That value does not take into consideration operational conditions or mitigation measures in place. The following columns should be added to the table of relative importance:

- Maintenance (patching, evaluating/testing patches, etc.) performed regularly for
  - Operating system
  - Hardware
  - Third-party software
  - Control system software
  - Customized software
- System monitoring frequency (how often is the system used/observed)
- System log (all logs) monitoring frequency
- Physical connections

The resulting table with values is shown in Table Atch1-3.

Table Atch1-3. Operational Considerations for Relative Importance

	A	I	J	K	L	M	N	O	P
1	Process / System Boundary	Operating System	Hardware	Third-Party Software	Control System	Customized Software	Monitoring Frequency	Log Monitoring Frequency	Connections
2	Mission								
3	Cyber System Mission	1	0	0	1	1	0.2	1	1
4	Backup Generator								
5	Fuel Supply								
6	Cyber System Fuel Supply	1	1	1	1	1	0.1	1	2
7	Cyber System Fuel Supply DMZ	0	1	1	0	1	0.4	1	2

Operating System	Value of 1 if this needs attention. Value of 0 if this is maintained and fully patched.
Hardware	Value of 1 if this needs attention. Value of 0 if this is maintained and fully patched.
Third-Party Software	Value of 1 if this needs attention. Value of 0 if this is maintained and fully patched.
Control System	Value of 1 if this needs attention. Value of 0 if this is maintained and fully patched.
Customized Software	Value of 1 if this needs attention. Value of 0 if this is maintained and fully patched.
Monitoring Frequency	Value based on the frequency of operations monitoring - Continuous: 0.1, Hourly: 0.2, Daily: 0.4, Weekly: 0.8, Monthly: 1.0, Yearly: 2.0, More: 4.0
Log Monitoring Frequency	Value based on the frequency of monitoring any logs - Continuous: 0.1, Hourly: 0.2, Daily: 0.4, Weekly: 0.8, Monthly: 1.0, Yearly: 2.0, More: 4.0
Connections	Number of interfaces. Console +1, Network (wired / wireless) +1, USB/Serial/Firewire/CDROM/DVD etc. +1 (max 3)

The calculation for the relative importance of interdependent systems (Zi) was the sum of the value of the dependencies shown as the yellow highlighted cell, C3 of Table Atch1-4.

Table Atch1-4. Subset of the Example Relative Importance of Interdependent Systems

	A	B	C	D	E	F	G	H
1	Process / System Boundary	GIS Data	Zi [=sum(D1...Dm)]	D1	D2	D3	D4	D5
2	Mission		1					
3	Cyber System Mission		=SUM(D3:H3)	=C2				

The table additions of columns I through P will be used in the calculation of the relative importance to mission modified by operational considerations. This value will be called the *Cyber Readiness*. Attention should be given to the entries with higher values.

An additional column should be added to the table so the calculations can be automated. For the purposes of this calculation, row 3 in the table will be used. All cells will be using this reference. C3 represents Zi.

Cyber Readiness
= Log10(C3) * sum(I3:M3) * N3 * O3 * P3

These values are then the risk prioritizations of the ICS/cyber components that support the functions with which missions rely. The higher values represent more at risk to the system. Some systems will have mitigations already in place, having the conversation with the system owner can determine if this is the case. The judgment of what resources to place should never be solely on the numeric value, however the numeric value can assist in making that determination.

The following tabular format checklist presents recommendations made earlier in the handbook using a modified DOTMLPF-F[37] construct. The checklist does not cover every last action that may be taken to secure installation ICS. Additional actions may be identified during assessment or even in the midst of implementation. Also, this is generic, meaning that applicability is broad rather than specific. Each installation will have differences, in some cases significant, in control systems architectures, security measures already in place, organizational and personnel management, and missions. The "one-size-fits-all" approach offered here will indeed yield a more secure ICS, but a closer fit will require tailoring (such as using other tools, requesting assistance of SMEs, etc.).

Actions are not listed in a particular order, except that policy should first be well-established so as to facilitate implementing actions in other areas. Nor do actions need to be implemented sequentially; many actions may be undertaken in parallel.

NOTE: A separate table may be used for each type of ICS or by mission supported.

The columns in the table are:
- FOCUS: COTMLPF-P area
- ACTION: ICS security action to implement
- COMMENTS: Notes/comments about that action
- PRI #:   Priority assigned to the action (self-defined priority scheme and criteria)
- POC: Person or office with primary responsibility for managing that action
- ASSGND: Date assigned by installation commander or ICS security team
- DONE: Date completed

Blank rows are included at the end of each "Focus" section for installation-specific additions.

---

[37] Modified by replacing the "D" with a "C" for cybersecurity.

TITLE <name of control system, infrastructure, or mission>

MISSION(S) SUPPORTED:

OTHER INFORMATION:

FOCUS	ACTION	COMMENTS	PRI #	POC	DATE ASSGND	DATE DONE
		POLICY				
P O L I C Y	Review ICS policy requirements with ICS Security Team					
	Review existing policy(ies) and amend/adopt as appropriate					
	Develop policy for the following:					
	• Roles & responsibilities (including vendors & third parties)					
	• Vulnerability & risk assessments					
	• Access control					
	• Security of assets					
	• Configuration control					
	• Acquisition of hardware & software					
	• Patch management					
	• Inventory accounting					
	• Education, training & exercises					
	Review ICS service level agreements with vendors and integrators	Changes to ICS systems often require vendor and/or integrator approval or support, which may not be covered in existing service level agreements				
	Set software and SDLC requirement	See the DHS Cyber Security Procurement				

	Action	Notes / Reference
	standards for ICS procurements	Language for Control Systems document, http://www.us-cert.gov/control_systems/pdf/FINAL-Procurement_Language_Rev4_100809.pdf
	Create incident response management plan with vendor, integrator, or third party ICS provider	Incident management across business boundaries, i.e. incident coordination with commercial energy providers, requires significant planning and cooperation; better to have the plan worked out before an incident occurs

LEADERSHIP

	Action	Notes
	Promulgate policies	
	Schedule awareness briefings for ICS managers, operators, & users	
	Attend stakeholder events	Gain and enhance situational awareness
	Collaborate with ICS vendors and service providers	Focus should be on security and training
	Develop new or adapt existing plans to address ICS. Plans include at least:	
	• Disaster Recovery	
	• System Security	
	• Contingency (include response to INFOCON, FPCON)	
	• Continuity of Operations	
	Add key ICS information to the Commander's Critical Information List	Think of most if not all ICS-related information as at least FOUO

L
E
A
D
E
R
S
H
I
P

PERSONNEL

P	Train all ICS managers, operators & users	Include policies, roles, security, incident response handling, etc.
E	Develop a refresher training program	
R	Perform background checks on everyone with ICS responsibility	
S	Require confidentiality or non-disclosure agreements	
O	Create an ICS incident response team	Can model on existing IT CERT or on DHS's ICS-CERT
N	Enforce system access controls	Includes network (logons) and physical (cipher-locked doors)
N	Maintain rosters for access to physical facilities	
E	Immediately delete all access (physical and system) of those who resign, retire, move, are fired, etc.	This must include third-party vendors, contractors, etc. as well as direct employees and military
L	Provide checklists/SOPs to each operator position as appropriate	Can be used also for training

TRAINING

T	Ensure ICS-specific training prior to granting individuals access	
R	Require IA training (initial & refresher) for all ICS managers, operators & users	In some cases, users of IT components of ICS are overlooked in IA training
A	Provide threat & vulnerability awareness via appropriate venues	
	Document all training; maintain currency	

Exercise ICS-related plans		
Include ICS in base-level exercises	For example, when INFOCONs are implemented or when FPCON is elevated	
ORGANIZATION		
Appoint an ICS IAM	Most installations with DOD networks already have an assigned IT network IAM; an ICS IAM is distinctly separate and trained specifically to ICS issues (but will coordinate with IT IAM)	
Assign responsibility for ICS configuration control		
Specify ICS roles & responsibilities of at least:		
• Commander		
• CEs/PWs		
• Communications/IT		
• Operations		
Identify leads for developing ICS-specific plans	Or for incorporating ICS considerations into existing plans	
Publish chain-of-command for incident response		
Identify roles & responsibilities of vendors, third parties		
FACILITIES		
Create a map/chart/topology of all	Include buildings, rooms, panels, cabling, etc.	

F	physical facilities	
A	Identify & inspect all physical facilities	
C	Develop a plan of action & milestones for correcting facility security deficiencies or weaknesses	
I		
L	Identify and secure portable assets	For example, fly-away kits, laptops, spares. Depict their locations on the facility map
I	Secure all cable terminations (their housings)	Wiring termination boxes often are located in isolated areas and with only minimum security controls (e.g., easily cut padlock, wire with lead breakage seal)
T		
I		
E		
S		

MATERIEL

M	Document the entire ICS infrastructure	Include logic diagrams, data flows, dependencies, and particularly connection to mission/mission support assets
A	Assign responsibility for accountability for physical assets	Include acquisition, configuration, inventory, etc.
T	Establish acquisition policy and process	
E	Require testing of any new component or program off-line	Always test before adding to the live infrastructure
R	Identify and control all ICS documentation and software media	
I	Ensure all replaced components are "cleaned" prior to disposition	
E	Provide failover or redundant servers and other components serving critical mission functions	
L		

CYBER SECURITY

Define & defend perimeters; approaches may include:	Part of a comprehensive defense-in-depth strategy		
• Segmentation			
• DMZs			
• Enclaves			
• VPNs to cross defended boundaries when necessary			
Control individual access:			
• Assign individual/unique logon IDs and passwords	Follow standard DOD practices		
• Design user access control architecture based on Least-User Access (LUA) model			
• Require role-based access control (RBAC)	For existing as well as new accounts		
• Disable all "guest" or anonymous accounts			
• Set UAC policy for event log auditing	ICS systems and applications are relatively static; any change to UAC configuration at the operating system, application, and data levels need to be identified immediately and reviewed for security implications		
• Set timeline and threshold monitoring requirements for UAC events	Event logs (functional and security) need to be reviewed in a timely manner; it will not do the teams any good if an IT IDS team reviews the alerts because the IDS team will not understand ICS traffic initially		
• Ensure functional UAC auditing and monitoring thresholds are put in place	Security-impacting changes to an ICS are more likely to be detected through functional incident evaluation rather than through		

C
Y
B
E
R

S
E
C
U
R
I
T
Y

CYBER SECURITY								
	security event monitoring; make sure ICS admins are reviewing their systems for security-impacting events							
• Ensure audit configuration and log monitoring on ICS systems can detect unusual egress traffic from privileged user accounts	As with previous comments, egress traffic from the ICS networks to the corporate/military or Internet need to be evaluated so a baseline of normal egress traffic can be established; unusual or anomalous egress traffic from privileged accounts needs to be identified and evaluated as quickly as possible							
Protect operating system:								
• Disable all unnecessary network services								
• Use (and keep current) virus-checking software	Virus detection programs may be difficult to update on live systems, and therefore will require diligence in maintaining currency							
• Establish software lifecycle management policy	Out-of-date software of any sort (firmware, operating system, third party/COTS, custom code, development frameworks, etc.) should all be maintained and within n or n-1 releases of a vendor's supported software							
• Enable audit logging & monitor								
• Remove all unnecessary programs								
• Implement security policies per vendor best security practices list	Security configurations should be done on each OS in addition to the external access controls like port configuration; this means disabling autorun, limiting remote registry access, etc.							
• Consider using IDS	If consider, do so judiciously and in close consultation with cybersecurity specialists who probably already had implemented an IDS on the IT network. Many IDS marketed							

CYBER SECURITY		
		specifically for ICS may not actually add more value to defense than already provided by the IT side IDS.
	Protect data:	
	• Encrypt data in motion (at least on the IT side)	Probably not able to encrypt data on the purely ICS component side, such as between a PLC and a master server; definitely unable to encrypt between a PLC and a sensor
	• Enforce controlled access to stationary data (files, databases, etc.)	
	• Back up system routinely and keep backups secure & accessible	A backup held exclusively by a vendor will not be "accessible" in certain circumstances, such as a FPCON Charlie or Delta
	• Implement separate data management procedures for business/ICS/operational data and data configuration files	Data segregation provides another security layer and helps prevent random failures of the OS/application from impacting data; since config files are often transferred from failing systems to the new system without being checked, malware authors hide RAT software in them
	• Map the flows of critical data at least annually to ensure data is being protected and accessed appropriately	Identify and map exactly where critical data goes throughout its usable life cycle to ensure you know exactly where it can be accessed and what protections are in place; use a data flow diagram and threat modeling tools to ensure appropriate trust boundaries and technical security controls are in place
	Control web services and Internet access:	
	• Disable unnecessary web services	
	• Use "white"/"black" lists	Whitelisting typically is favored over blacklisting; situational determination required

CYBER SECURITY	
• Enforce acceptable-use policy on Internet access and browsing	
• Use a web application firewall (WAF) if possible	Put a WAF in between the ICS network and other networks to ensure known attacks can be blocked before they hit vulnerable endpoints. In most cases, adequate web content and service filtering cannot be adequately performed at the host level on an ICS network server or endpoint; the static nature of ICS networks make the WAF easier to implement
• Implement best security practices per browser vendor	OS security is not sufficient to defend against endpoint attacks over port 80; browser level security controls need to be put in place as well
• Use native browser tools and third party browser security applications	Use of tools like NoScript or BetterPrivacy prevent automatic execution of scripts within the browser and prevent auto-execution of malware via browser components or web services
• Develop and implement web component and services software development lifecycle	Web service and web component attacks against the browser are a big deal; browser plug-ins, extensions, and services must be controlled to prevent attack methodologies such as JIT spraying, ROP, etc.
• Perform web app security scans before and after web services are enabled on servers and hosts	Use of web-based services presents a significant attack surface on servers and hosts; ensure a baseline of those services has been performed so any security gaps can be identified
• Incorporate web app security touchpoints into the standard development lifecycle of all web-enabled software	Make sure vendors, integrators, and in-house development teams are testing their web apps and have a mature software security development program for any software deployed on a system

		Keep malware from hooking into systems or gaining access via long term cookie and data storage by web services
	• Configure systems to deny long-term storage of web service information like cookies and temporary cache	
	Identify and manage all network communication access points; disable those not needed and protect all others	
	• Modems/dial-up	
	• Wireless	
	• Cable/DSL	
	• Fiber-optic	
	• Satellite	
	• Ethernet	
	• Cellular	
	Identify and manage all removable media access points; disable those not needed and protect all others	
	• Mobile devices (cell phones, MP3 players)	
	Removable hard drive storage devices (SAN disks, USB thumb drives, flash drives)	
	Identify and manage all messaging service access points; disable those not needed and protect all others	
	• SMS/MMS text messaging	
	• VoIP	

C Y B E R S E C U R I T Y

C Y B E R	• Instant messaging	
	• Unified communications solutions	
	• Intranet server resources (SMB messenger service, remote registry, etc.)	
	Identify and manage all remote management applications, services, or functions, disable those not needed and protect all others	
S E C U R I T Y	• Web management interfaces	Web management interfaces exist for systems from the firmware on up to the data layer of the OSI model; every one of them need to be identified and secured
	• Remote hardware management tools	
	• Asset management and configuration software	
	• ⬚ost-based security software (A⬚, ⬚IPS, back up services, etc.)	
	Ensure there are no "hidden" or "backdoor" access capabilities	

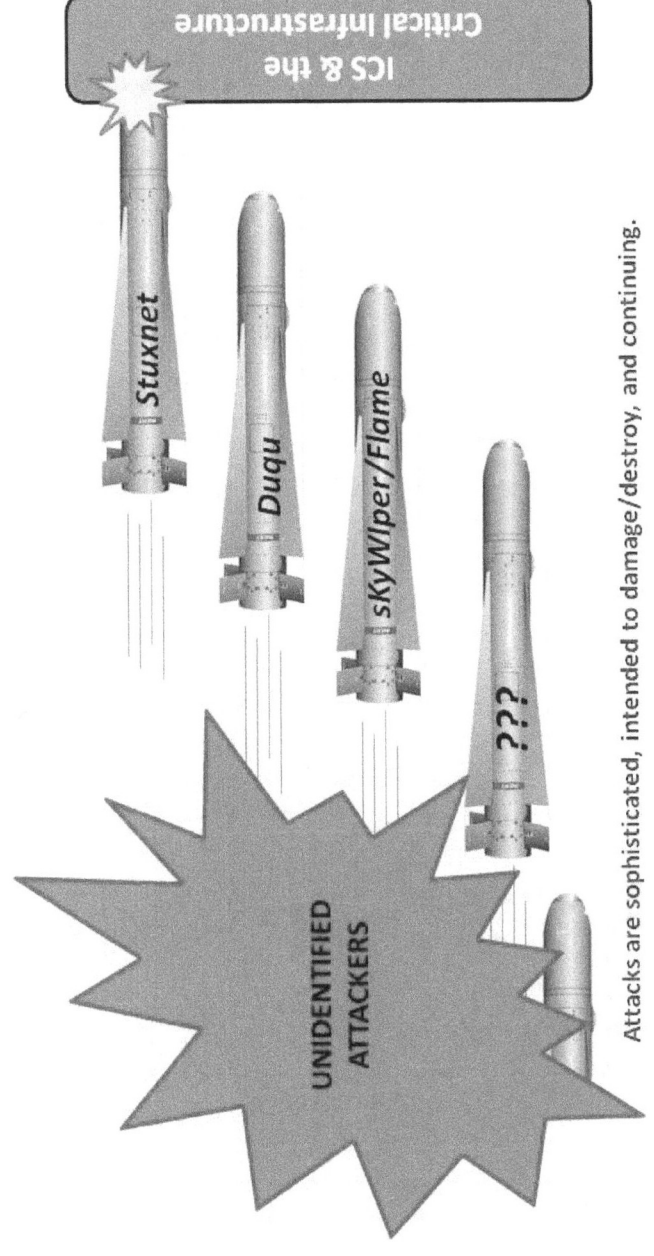

ICS & the
Critical Infrastructure

Stuxnet

Duqu

sKyWIper/Flame

???

UNIDENTIFIED
ATTACKERS

Attacks are sophisticated, intended to damage/destroy, and continuing.